"I don't know any other book quite like this [...] touched and charmed would be an understatement. A love of many kinds of music fuses here with warmth for many kinds of people. And with acute affection for all the surprises that music and people can bring."

Greg Sandow, Graduate Studies faculty, Juilliard

"Sales is service. If you don't believe that, this book will change your mind."

Doc Searls, co-author, *The Cluetrain Manifesto*

"Call it *Diary of a Record Salesman* except that doesn't do this personal journey justice. Real, honest and poignant, not something you find every day in a business book."

Seth Godin, author, *Linchpin*

"Having both done our time on the CD selling floor, Joe Zitt and I can tell you: On the front lines of retail, the folks on the floor often feel like cannon fodder. I came through it with PTSD; Joe came out of it with a book that could revolutionize selling in the same way Sam Pocker's *Retail Anarchy* changed buyers. From Karajan to Kate Bush, from Drag Queens in the Christmas spirit to distractible little old ladies who know exactly what they want, in Joe's version of '19th Nervous Breakdown,' when he sings, 'Here it comes,' he's talking about a sale. *Kerching!*"

Hank Bordowitz, author, *Dirty Little Secrets of the Record Business*

"Zitt has a good eye for the absurd, and the humorous nature to navigate it. This is not blog imitating life, but life imitating blog."

Rabbi Rami Shapiro, author, *The Sacred Art of Lovingkindness*

19th Nervous Breakdown
Making Human Connections in the Landscape of Commerce

19th Nervous Breakdown

*Making Human Connections
in the Landscape of Commerce*

Joseph Zitt

BLACK ANGEL PRESS

To the workers and customers
of store 57,
and to all those
who serve to connect people
with the art and information
that they love.

Contents

Contents

Contents

The Path of Sales

Close your eyes and think of the word "salesman." What comes to mind?

- The way that Pee-Wee Herman would scream "Salesmen!" whenever one would come to the Playhouse?

- The stereotypical used car salesman, brandishing tricks and lies to dump a clunker on the unsuspecting?

- Willy Loman, schlepping toward death?

With such images in our minds, it's no surprise that we shy away from dealing with other people when we buy things. Browsing the web stores alone, online, does have its benefits. But when we do this, the direct human experience of shopping is lost.

In the best of shopping experiences, in person, in stores, we work with guides who strive to connect us with the things that we desire and will come to love. The best salespeople listen mindfully to what we want and need. They pick up on what we say and how we say it. But they listen as well as to the spaces of the unsaid that suggest new areas, items, or experiences that we don't yet know.

Online shops can show us lists of recommendations. They build these from mathematical models, derived from the purchases of people who have bought what we have bought, and from the opinions of people who say that they like what we have said that we like. But without the live human connection, we miss the possibility of human empathy. We miss the intuitions that leap outside of logic to the unexpected things that turn out to be just what we need.

The writers of *The Cluetrain Manifesto* said in 1999 that "Markets are conversations." Even more than that, buying and selling in person creates relationships, as real (if more fleeting and not necessarily as intense) as those that we have in families, in romance, and in our careers. The best salespeople learn to honor and cherish these relationships as carefully as the other important relationships in our lives.

I am a salesman. It seems strange to say it (and I don't think I'd ever said it myself before typing that sentence just now), but I am a salesman, and have been for close to a decade now. When I started on this unintended second career, a coworker told me, "If you last through three Christmases, you're a lifer." I just survived my ninth Christmas at the store. I guess I'm here to stay.

In my first career, for the first twenty years of my working life, I wrestled with computers, as a technical writer, editor, and programmer. But when that world and I parted ways with the collapse of the first dot.com boom, I discovered that I needed to work directly with people, rather than with machines. And when I stumbled onto the path of the salesperson, I knew that I had found my place in the world.

Customers have told me that I approach selling books and music like a ministry. Sometimes I find what people want. I hope that sometimes I find them what they need. And helping the store make a profit is probably a good thing, too.

In my work, in my life, I look for human contact, for communication, for the chance to help people leave the store happier than when they came in. Here are some of the stories of some of these people, and what happened when our lives crossed on the floor of one large and often crazy store.

A New Career In a New Town

11 November 2002

I'd been helping out a friend with a tiny record label, getting organized, duping CD-Rs, and the like. On Thursday, there was a rush
to get disks ready for and delivered to a musician in San Francisco
who was heading out on tour the next day. So I burned the discs
at the label owner's house, then brought the packaging home and
put it together there.

I made the contact with the musician without a problem. He
was running around the city, so we arranged to meet at the cafe at
a large bookstore downtown. He got there at about 9:20 PM and
was very appreciative that we had the disks ready.

I had a comfortable evening, once out of the rain, mostly reading
the new *Cambridge Companion to John Cage* (woohoo!) and the
new *Wired* issue focusing on science and religion.

Chapter 2

After a while, I wandered up to the CD department, and, over-heard a woman with an indeterminable accent driving the sales folk nuts. She was trying to find "a big famous classical music song, it is called 'Song About Happiness' by Beethoven and Cara John."

After hearing them flap about helplessly, I went over and told them that I might be able to help, and asked her to repeat her request. "Did it sound something like this?" I asked, and sang the first couple of lines of the Ode to Joy.

"Yes! Yes! It is it!" (she practically bounced up and down).

"OK," I said. "It's the Ode to Joy, the last movement of Beethoven's Ninth Symphony. You probably are looking for a recording conducted by Herbert Von Karajan—that's with a K—and I think there's at least one on Deutsche Grammophon."

The sales guy, who was on the phone trying to get help, wandered over, still tethered to the phone, and pulled out a copy and handed it to her. "Hey, some guy here just figured it out," he said on the phone, then hung up.

After she wandered off, I followed him over to the counter. "Man, I would never have gotten that!" he said.

I hit him with the inevitable question, "So are you guys hiring in the music department?"

His eyes got kinda wide. "You interested?"

I nodded. "Dude, we so are looking for a classical guy!" He looked around and spotted someone in the distance. "There's my manager!" he yelled, and went running across the store. I followed. He pulled another man with a badge out of the employee area. "Dude, this is the dude that got the classical question. You still hiring?"

The guy said, "Yeah! You want to work here?"

I said, "That could be good."

So we talked for a few minutes, and we set up an interview for Saturday afternoon at 1 PM. He asked if I wanted part time or full time (I said full time would be great, but part time would be possible), how much I was looking to earn (I said that I knew the pay wasn't huge, but that I guessed that it would be sufficient), and if I had worked in a record store before (no, but that may not be much of a problem).

So I spent Friday afternoon turning into Classical Guy. I filled out a fresh application with that focus, and headed over to another store in the chain to get a good sense of what they stock and to bone up on what was happening in the latest classical magazines and the like. I figured that I could probably bluff my way through much of this, but I'm pretty rusty, having fallen out of touch with the stuff from that little bit of time preceding 1950 or so.

The interview on Saturday went quickly. I focused on being interested in customer service (after all, I was the weird kid who wanted to be a reference librarian when he grew up). He didn't ask me any questions about classical music, because he didn't know a lot about classical himself.

He then had me interview immediately with the Human Resources person, which also went well. She asked me a lot of obligatory questions, like whether I understood that not showing up for a shift causes real havoc. It turns out that they get a significant number of young workers who have never quite wrestled with that concept.

She also asked me if I listened to other music, and I talked about the range of other stuff that I listen to, and mentioned that I had been thumbing through the Pete Seeger rack in the folk section before the interview. It turns out we're both fans of his group The Weavers. She was impressed that I could name the members and sing a bit of a Holly Near song, "Hay Una Mujer Desaparecida," that they covered.

She ran through the benefits as they would be available. I would be a Seasonal Temp through January 5th, with the benefits that part-time workers get, then would kick into full benefits if I would be kept on after that. That interview went pretty quickly too, and the manager said I would hear from him by midweek.

Apparently they didn't need even that much time to decide: I got the call at 10:30 Sunday morning. I'll be starting with training Wednesday morning, then be doing 25-30 hours a week for a while. At the starting rate of pay (about 20% of what I was getting at my last job), I should be able to scrape by.

This came together through one heck of a combination of luck and chutzpah. The Spiritual Director that I've been seeing (like a psychotherapist, except that she talks in terms of religion rather than, well, psychotherapy) has had me looking at the wild set of coincidences and odd bits of timing that have brought me out here and put me in a position to do a lot of what I'd been wanting to do, as well as to refocus my life away from the computer work that I'd burned out on and toward new things. She says that, no matter how anthropomorphic an image one chooses to use or not use, it's in these coincidences toward good that one can "see God" in life. I don't know that I'm ready to see in those terms, but it's at the very least a strong metaphor.

More stuff is happening, but I should get to sleep. I have a few days to get out of night-owl mode and get used to being awake during the day.

In the Moment

16 Novombor 2002

Well, I've survived my first part-of-a-week on the new job. Lots of picking up skills, many of which many other people have had since they were quite young, but I'd never encountered.

Prime among them is working cash registers and dealing with customers at them. Fortunately, most customers are being rather merciful as I fumble through their purchases.

The prompts on the register screens guide us through most steps in order, but some parts can be sort of random, such as trying to decide how to juggle handling change or credit cards, taking media out of the plastic security holders, demagnetizing the security "chiclets," and bagging the items. I still have yet to get that into a flow. But I understand that that will come with time.

There's an interesting aspect of "living in the moment" to working the registers. Each interaction with a customer takes on the order of a minute. Once the customer steps away, you're pretty much (barring any major screw-ups being brought back to you) tabula rasa as far as dealing with the next. And the next. And the next. Ad infinitum ad (at least) Christmas.

The Acme Catastrophe Generator

20 November 2002

Another challenging but fun day at work. I think I may have set a new record for the number of things going wrong in a single transaction.

Working the registers today, I had to do things for real customers that I had only done in training, and developed brain-lock on how to do several of them. Fortunately, there were coworkers around to help with most of those cases.

The biggest mess came on a transaction early in the day. An older couple were buying three calendars (replete with cutesy pictures of cats) and had a coupon of a type that I'd never seen. The calendars didn't have the usual tags with item identifiers on them, but did have other bar codes that I tried scanning. No dice. I called for a manager, and the Chief Big Honcho Manager of the entire store showed up. He pointed out that there were actually two unrelated bar codes on the calendars and that I was consistently scanning the wrong one (error #1). Once I scanned them, I rang up the sale— then realized that I'd forgotten to scan the coupon (error #2). So I had to have the manager cancel that transaction. I then rang it up again with the coupon, which, having been put in slightly incorrectly (the scanner is very finicky), jammed the scanner (error #3). Once we managed to retrieve that, we got everything to print out correctly, and finished things —except that the eagle-eyed customer spotted that we had given him the receipt for the canceled transaction rather than the good one (error #4).

Fortunately, the customer and manager were good natured and patient. The manager reminded me that it's much better to be hitting these problems now than a month from now when we expect that the store will be an utter frenzied zoo.

I had a bizarre and almost catastrophic occurrence this evening. Along my walking route home from the BART station, there's an array of newspaper boxes, mostly for the free local papers. Since I hadn't picked up the Daily Planet (yes, the Berkeley Daily Planet. Really.) in the morning, I opened the paper-box and got one. The door slammed shut heavily, since there's one hell of a spring holding it shut. As it turns out, at least some of the boxes are not nailed down. With the force of the door shutting, the Daily Planet box shifted back slightly. This knocked the box of the SF Weekly, which must have been poised precariously at the edge of the curb, into the street. As it fell over, it yanked on the chain that connected it to the Daily Planet box, which followed it into the street, scooting around it and into the flow of traffic. And lo, there was heard in the land much screeching of brakes and sounding of horns. By some miracle, no one hit anything. I was able to drag the boxes to the curb, though not back up onto it.

I think Wile E. Coyote must have days like these...

Colony: Dry By a Brook

14 January 2003

I'm really enjoying working in the CD department. Coworkers are good, I get to use various skills I've acquired, and I even kinda like commuting—I've gotten to do a lot more reading than I had been doing, now that I'm spending a significant amount of time riding on and waiting for trains.

We've had the usual array of wacky customers. It got so that I recognized a certain look on the face of an oncoming drag queen, and to have a copy of *The Most Fabulous Christmas Ever* with Eartha Kitt's rendition of "Santa Baby" already in hand.

My favorite odd request came from someone who wanted a piece of music that he'd heard on the radio. He'd written it down as "Colony: Dry by a Brook." It took some tries to get what it was: in the flurry of questions, he said that it was a classical piece for solo cello, and sounded "kinda Jewish." I took him to a listening station, and dialed up one of the tracks from it. Sure enough, it was what I expected: "Kol Nidre" by Bruch.

Waiting for a Friend

19 January 2003

An exhausting and exhilarating day, mostly spent in a protest march in San Francisco.

After the march, we met up with a friend of ours at my store's coffee shop. I got to show my friends my workplace, and helped her select a CD of the Brandenburg Concertos for a friend.

(While I was there, one coworker (let's call her Rose) took me aside and said in her solemn explanatory way: "You know, Joe, it is possible, on days when you're not working, to visit places other than your workplace and experience other people." But I told her that the person whom we had met lived just a few blocks away, and that I had stayed up all night worrying about the CDs that I had left on the cart unshelved. She realized that I was kidding about the second part... I think.)

Precision

25 February 2003

I think I got one of the ultimate questions at work yesterday. An older man with what I heard as a German accent told me, very slowly, "I am looking for an... album that... I heard an... advertisement on the... radio for an... album... I do not remember the name of the... band and I do not remember any of the songs... but I... believe that the name of the album was... Best of." After some prodding, he came up with three things that it may have been like: Jefferson Airplane, Emerson Lake and Palmer, and Earth Wind and Fire. Well, that let us know that whatever he was looking for was probably somewhere in our massive Rock & Pop section. Or maybe R&B. If not Folk or Jazz.

Invasion of the Snotty Bastards

15 March 2003

The consensus at work today was that some sort of fog of nastiness had hit San Francisco, resulting in a sudden inexplicable torrent of the crankiest, surliest customers seen in a long time. This was coupled with a massive spike in the number of attempted shopliftings thwarted at the store (no idea about successful ones).

The nadir for me: a young guy came up the escalator, look around, and said "I'm seeing Jazz, I'm seeing Blues... ?" I told him that Rock, Pop, and the rest are around the other side of the escalators. He said "Oh, the stuff that's after your time." Resisting the urge to spank him, I opened my arms wide and said "I think of it all as 'during'."

Later, the Southpaw (always the best of the workers at thinking up snappy comebacks, though gentle about deploying them), came up with what I should have said: "Oh, you're looking for children's music. That's on the third floor."

We had people cursing out employees in the elevators, thrown merchandise, people refusing to pay sales tax because they don't have it in the state in which they live, and situations in the bathrooms that I will refrain from describing. Ugh.

But there were some good things, too. As always, the best part of the job is hooking people up with the music they love. Usually it's not particularly challenging stuff, but it's what they need at the time. Today a woman was quite grateful that I was able to locate a copy of Mary McGregor's "Torn Between Two Lovers"; last week I was able to find another customer the exact Doris Day album with which she had grown up.

Plunking against the Drunks

26 March 2003

We had a few classic customers this weekend. One was appalled that we didn't have the Schoenberg *War Requiem* (er, that's because it's by Benjamin Britten).

Another browbeat us for several minutes about finding an album of many different versions of "Amazing Grace" before saying "Oh, wait, I meant 'Danny Boy'."

And an imperious woman, fur-bedecked with a thick Russian accent, berated us for, well, just about everything not being up to her standards. "Every time I am coming in here and you do not have what I need and I cannot listen to it. You are the worst store in city. I keep coming in here and you can never get anything." When I finally convinced her to order the disc with the obscure song she was looking for, I saw that she was a frequent customer and ordered from us often. Go figure.

Busman's Holiday

16 April 2003

I've had a busy couple of days back home in New Jersey, riding around with my father on various errands (partially to stay out from underfoot as my stepmother went into the traditional frenzy preparing for the Seder). Today we dropped into our store in Wayne, NJ, ostensibly to find one more haggadah. (When I counted them in the basement we were short by one, but there mysteriously were enough by the time of the seder itself. It's either a miracle or a reminder never to trust my own eyes in counting things.)

The computer that customers could use at their store was down, but I introduced myself to a clerk as being from another store and he let me use the employee-only search system. We determined that the store didn't have any of it, and since the link to the whole "sister store" network was out, so I couldn't check others nearby. It turns out, curiously, that the clerk had previously worked at our store in Mission Viejo, CA, at which, if I recall, our General Manager and another coworker also had worked.

We spent some time in the café. (No, I didn't try to use my employee discount, since the folks behind the counter seemed a bit stressed already.) My father got quite annoyed that they appeared to be ignoring him as he stood by the baked goods display. I realized that the café had an unfortunate design bug: from where they were standing, he was hidden by a pillar. But that's not something that could be fixed easily.

It's been good spending time with my father. He's moving kind of slowly nowadays, both physically and in responding to things, but not to a upsetting degree. He wants very much for me to move back east to be with him, but I really feel like I'm where I need to be and doing what I need to do living in Berkeley and working in San Francisco.

Chapter 3

Freude, schoene Grandfunkrailroad

29 April 2003

The single craziest customer complaint that I've heard yet came on Sunday: A customer attempted to explain to me, in long-suffering terms, that Beethoven's Choral Symphony was a strictly instrumental work until Billy Joel wrote the lyrics to the Ode to Joy. And she demanded to know why we only carried recordings that had that horrific German translation.

But on the flip side, I got some pleasing news: the store just instituted an Employee of the Month award, and I'm the first recipient. This gets me little other than bragging rights and a $25 gift card, along with pleasant razzing by my coworkers.

It's funny to realize that, while everyone on my previous job bitched wildly and started heading for the exits when the company stopped providing catered lunches everyday and taking us out to dinner and drinks several times a week, on this job getting a $25 gift card means a lot to me. And while that amount might have covered a dinner at a not-too-expensive restaurant for me not long ago, I find myself calculating whether I can stretch the card to cover a month of weekend lunches.

It also helps that I've been winning a free lunch each week pretty consistently for being one of the only three or four employees to get at least ten percent of our customers to give us their email addresses when they check out. Oddly and unfortunately, this is compromised by the amount of repeat customers that I've been getting, since each can only toss his address in once, and those that don't drive the percentages down. Ah, well.

Mathis der Brawler

6 May 2003

Yesterday, for the first time, a customer actually threw something at me. He was obviously a bit crazed already, and went off the deep end when he had misread a card and believed that we had a boxed set behind the information desk rather than the registers. When I told him it wasn't there but up front, he grabbed the bin card with the artist's name from the bin (and yes, the card said that the box set was at the registers), and winged it at me, cursing, and stomped off.

The artist he was so upset about? Johnny Mathis. Maybe the guy really needed a daily dose of crooning to keep him calm. When I told my housemate about this, he pointed out that it seemed like the guy was already angry about something else, and I just happened to be in his path.

I May Not Be There When You Want Me (But I'm Right On Time)

1 July 2003

The day started, as usual for a Tuesday, with my getting up at a fairly comfortable hour and heading into San Francisco to start work at 1 PM. I got in right at 12:59, clocked in, turned around to look at the schedule to see whether I'd start the day at the information desk, at the register, or working on my section—and saw that I wasn't on the schedule at all. I clocked back out, went to a nearby manager to find out what was going on, and got another peak into the wackiness of the corporate mind.

I'm scheduled to work on Friday, July 4, which (for either of you who might not have known) is a national holiday in the US. As a sort of reward for coming in on that day, those who do get an additional day off. Now, I had figured that that meant that we would have a day added to the pool of personal days that we could take during the year, but that wasn't so. Instead, as far as I understand it, each of us had been given a paid day off for one of the days that we worked during the week. Today was mine. It had been marked as such on the schedule, but I (and at least one coworker) had missed it and come in anyway. So, with an unusual number of employees taking vacation this week, and a huge number of tourists vacationing in town coming to our store, we end up even further shorthanded. I dropped upstairs to see how things were doing in my area, and found someone from another department getting utterly flustered trying to handle things. I helped direct customers and answer some questions for a few minutes until backup arrived, but I couldn't help her out at the register since that would mean logging myself as the employee for transactions at a time that I wasn't clocked in, which would raise all sorts of bureaucratic havoc.

On the Spot

13 July 2003

At work, managers occasionally give out "On the Spot" Customer Service Evaluation forms when they see employees doing things unusually well (or badly). Yesterday, I got three: different managers (including the General Manager) heard me recommending further purchases to customers, as we'd been told to do, and apparently were impressed. They said that while it sounds forced for a lot of people, when I do it, it sounds like normal conversation.

The thing is, for me that *is* normal conversation. I'm always recommending music to people, and since my mind is a writhing mass of music trivia connected by soundbites, I can almost always think of something related to what a person is buying. (Actually, in two cases, I pulled a total blank based on a customer's purchases, so I turned it around and asked each customer what he would recommend to someone who liked that disk—and then was able to make links from those recommendations to stuff that I knew.)

When I'm at work, I am, in a sense, performing in the role of Music Guy, conversationally and in action. Doing it at work has immediate and real feedback. Much of what I do is rather scored, too, with a series of actions that have to take place in a certain order.

And I can get really messed up when that order is interrupted. Fortunately, since I do things in a pretty standardized way at the register, I can usually backtrack if something's awry, get back to the step where I get thrown off, and restart from there. Today, however, I got completely off-course when a manager started "helping" me by doing some of the later steps in parallel to my earlier steps. When I got an error on the register, things were not where I had put them, and I couldn't quite figure out the state of the situation. As usually happens, I got flustered and started getting more errors in trying to recover from those errors, to the point that I had to just back off and let the manager finish the transaction. I also, as often happens, messed up the following transaction in trying to regain equilibrium from that one.

Fortunately, the managers are consistently good, and willing to fix things. And I guess they figure that the things that I do well balance the screw-ups.

Making a List and Checking It Twice

5 September 2003

A few days ago, a customer bought a DVD of a gory horror movie and an Englebert Humperdinck CD. When I joked about the odd combination, he said, "They're not both for me—this piece of crap is for someone else." Unfortunately, I didn't see him gesture, so

I have no idea which of the two he considered to be the piece of crap. Both are equally plausible.

I got a call at work a couple of days ago asking if several CDs were available. As the person on the phone worked his way down the list, I realized that he was reading from the selection of CDs that a local critic had picked as the best recordings of the operas that the local opera company would be doing. When I asked him if this was so, he admitted that he was an editor from the critic's paper, and was checking up on the list, since they'd gotten letters that complained that the recommended CDs were out of print. I said, in his defense, that at least one was the only recording of that work, and that others were widely available though out of print. But I was pleased that the editor had chosen to check with us as his authority as to what was in print. I also gave him a quick lesson as to how to check via the Web on exactly the same database that I was checking via our intranet.

Some Devil

3 October 2003

Coming into work, I saw a poster for Dave Matthews's upcoming CD, *Some Devil*. I mentioned to Rose that I had immediately read the title backward, saw it as "live demos" and wondered if that was what's on the disc. She asked me if I always read things backward. Thinking of it later, I realize that i don't do it for all text, but primarily when I run across really arbitrary strings like that title.

Later, I happened to speak to a representative from Matthews's record company, who called us asking for our hunches as to why people were or weren't buying the disc. I mentioned the reversed title and what it suggested. She seemed quite startled, and said that she hadn't noticed it or heard anyone mention it. I told her that it had initially suggested to me that the album might be an "odds and sods" collection of tracks that the band hadn't gotten around to doing, and wondered if anyone else was having that impression. (Looking now, I see that the name comes from the title and lyric to one of the songs on the disc. Which I still haven't heard.)

CHAPTER 4

"He's told us not to blow it/Cause he knows it's all worthwhile"

10 February 2004

Sometimes it seems that the store has some sort of force field keeping people there—many of my coworkers who live in the neighborhood drop through anyway on days that they are not working. Much of our social lives, and many of our connections in other endeavors, all tie into the people from the store. It could seem constricting, but is, I think, a sign of the generally relaxed atmosphere (even considering the pressure-cooker atmosphere of days with lots of customers).

Sometimes the laid-back feeling can present problems. One coworker today told me that she had recently made an uncharacteristic wisecrack at a customer, in a way that would have never happened elsewhere, and which the customer did not take well.

And we sometimes have a tendency to cluster at the information booths and hang out. But we are mostly kind of compulsive about customer service—it's not unusual for us to break off a conversation with a coworker mid-sentence to offer help to a passing customer. The customers, while not always right, always come first. It does mean, however, that it can take several conversations to complete an anecdote.

Today I spent quite a bit of time helping one customer who was looking for music from an album by Chicago that he was sure had never been released on CD. I managed to track down release information for the CD (including a picture of the cover). Even though we wouldn't be able to get it for him, I got him as much information as I could. (One of my mantras at work: "If we can't get you the music, we'll at least get you closer to it.") It turned out that he was working in some capacity with a very well-known band and was hoping to convince them to cover a track from that CD. I would be quite pleased to have been part of that process.

We can check a couple of different computer systems to see if an item is in stock. The database is, however, only updated each evening, and there are a few situations (such as when items are stolen) that can lead to false positive results. When I look up an item in the system and the computer says that we have it, I tell the customer "the computer is optimistic," and go to see if we can actually find it on the shelves. This usually amuses them, and keeps me from disappointing them too badly if the item isn't actually there.

I got a commendation yesterday from my bosses for my work. I was called away from the registers and into a meeting with them, and I feared that I'd done something wrong, but instead they had me sign a letter of commendation that they had written to go in my file, praising my attitude, knowledge, and intuitive.

I suspect that part of what helps me do things well is my constant worry that I'm screwing things up. It keeps me on my toes, and always looking for ways to do things better. Some of my coworkers continually flout rules, and are peeved when called on it. I always figure that I'm about to get caught violating some rule that I've never heard of before, so I'm pretty exacting about following the ones that I know.

When I was young, I could never quite figure out what the rules were for things (and the ground rules for social interactions still mystify me), and I was always getting caught doing something wrong. I still get a small sense of dread when I hear someone coming up the stairs or down the hall toward my room, sensing that "the grownups" are about to yell at me for something. And I'm still very timid in dealing with authority figures—it takes a lot of girding my courage to drop downstairs to pay my rent.

I ran an underground newspaper in fifth grade (yes, in fifth grade —this was 1969, and such things were in the air). At first we wrote it up on those blue copier stencils (were those mimeographs, or did that word refer to something else?) and had a teacher reproduce them for the class. When the teachers stopped cooperating (I forget why), we still wrote them up on the stencils and, the school being small enough to make this feasible, passed the physical stencil itself around.

The one article that I recall writing for the paper (which, I now recall, was named *The Printed Word*, except for one issue which we called *The Skylark* from a quote from Kahlil Gibran) was titled "Okay, But First." Its thesis was that no matter what a kid would try to do, thinking that he had gotten permission, a grownup would always find a way to make it dependent on one more unexpected chore.

Some years later, in high school, I had a job once a week in a lawyer's office, replacing pages in law books with pages showing changes in the law that week. This lawyer only dealt with a very specific area of bond trading, within the state of New Jersey. There were still enough changes to the law to keep me busy swapping pages for a couple of hours each week. This helped convince me that whoever and wherever you are, you're probably in violation of some law that you never heard of, and the Powers That Be can probably nail you for it at any time.

Whipped Cream and Other Delights

13 February 2004

Overheard today in the café:
   Customer: Medium low-fat cappuccino, please?
   Barista: What's your whipped cream option?
   Customer (with a deer-in-the-headlights look): What?
   Barista: Your options are "Yes," "No," "A Little," or "Extra."
   Customer: Well, I'm getting low-fat, so maybe I can get a little. (pause) Or maybe I should switch to soy milk and get the normal. (pause) Or I could leave out the milk entirely and get an espresso con panna. Or... (looks increasingly helpless).
   Barista: Can I boil that down to "Yes"?
   Customer: (nods, relieved)

Spirits and Dreams

16 February 2004

This felt like a very long day. Fortunately, there wasn't the expected torrent of returns of valentine gifts. Still, it seemed like the customers were weirder and more demanding than usual.

I had one delightful question at the end of the day, though. A woman was preparing to run some groups about dreams, and needed songs about dreams to set the mood as people entered. We came up with a whole list of possibilities, and I sold her an Everly Brothers album for "All I Have to Do is Dream" and the soundtrack to Walt Disney's *Cinderella* for "A Dream is a Wish the Heart Makes." She was quite pleased and said that she'd be returning for more.

When I brought my supervisor over to my section to show him an experiment that I was trying in labeling the bins for opera CDs, I saw that a large bottle of cheap vodka had been left in a nook under the Naxos CDs. When he turned to me from looking at the tags, he saw me holding the vodka bottle, and got a very confused look. We quickly spirited it over to the information desk and threw it away. I suspect it wouldn't have made for much of a party anyway.

Birds on the Wire

18 February 2004

At the store, we looped a DVD of early Beatles performances and newsreels where yesterday we had been playing Hitchcock's *The Birds*. From across the floor, the shrieking of overwrought teenagers sounded exactly the the screech of the birds' attacks.

This evening, one of our less clueful workers asked me why they kept putting out new recordings of older works, when, say, everything by Beethoven had certainly been recorded already. I tried to explain to him the differences in interpretation of mostly-fixed scores. This required going into the differences between classical and most popular musics: most music that he was familiar with required a fixed tempo and a very narrow dynamic range. In most classical music, however, especially in the Romantic era, there's a lot of flexibility possible in these areas: with the use of rubato, for example, one can speed up some parts of a phrase and slow others down, as long as they more or less add up to the general tempo. Similarly, classical music can, within a piece, very much more widely in volume than popular musics tend to (when a popular piece seems to be getting louder and softer, it's usually changing the density and timbre of sounds rather than the actual volume).

I tried a couple analogies, by pointing out to him the differences in how different people would play the same blues (though my attempts to point him to John Lee Hooker and Sonny Terry didn't work, since he hadn't heard of them). I think I finally got through by talking about the different portrayals of *Hamlet*, with Laurence Olivier, Mel Gibson, and Ethan Hawke playing the same lines very differently. Since he's somewhat of a movie fiend, he appeared to get this.

Right On That Shore

21 February 2004

I had the opening shift at work today, I set my backup alarm clock and woke up at 6:45 AM. I like waking up early in the morning. I also like staying up late. The two tend to conflict. (Or, as a friend told me in the 80's, "You're a morning person and a night person. You're just no good in the afternoons.")

One customer today was looking for some music that he had heard last year at Grace Cathedral. We were able to find out from him that it was sung by a choir from England and that one of the songs had something to do with Jerusalem. He kept spinning out into anecdotes. Several hinged on a friend of his, whose father had worked with Diego Rivera, as he told us identically three times.

Another insisted that we find him an album named *Songs of France*, "with exactly that title!" Flipping through the French music, I didn't see it, but told him that I did see *Music of France*. "Yes!" he bellowed, "It's exactly that title!"

The funniest was a woman who was looking for a couple of very specific things. One was Tina Turner's greatest hits album. Another was a recording of Marilyn Horne singing "Shall We Gather at the River." We found the Horne easily. As we headed toward the Turner bin, I recommended that she try the complete Copland cycle of songs. She replied, "No, I've come in for these two very specific things, and I have to keep focused on—Ooh! Dinah Shore! You have Dinah Shore! I must get some of these!" Her husband and I both grinned as she dug through the Shore collections like a feral cat discovering a discarded turkey dinner.

Freeze Frame

22 February 2004

My favorite exchange of the day:
    Customer: I haven't been able to ever to find this out, but could you dig up who recorded the song "Harper Valley PTA"?
    Me (instantly): Jeannie C. Riley.
    Customer: You frighten me.
    Me: I had the 45.
    At one point we were playing an Elvis Presley disc over the overhead play system. When it was playing "Treat Me Nice," I saw several people tapping their feet, bopping in place as they flipped through the CDs, and playing air guitar. As the song hit its sudden dramatic silences, the whole group (who weren't watching each other) would do an abrupt freeze frame, moving again when the music returned.

Walking In Rhythm

24 February 2004

Flash Impact saved my butt this evening at work. I was dealing with some Japanese customers and having no luck figuring out what they wanted. I finally got them to wait a moment, went to the schedule, saw that Flash Impact was working, and paged him. He sounded a little panicky as I described the situation to him on the phone, but he valiantly came up the stairs (even though he was on lunch), translated for the customers, got them what they wanted, and rang up the sale.

Once they were gone, he proceeded to collapse on the floor behind the register, his blue hair resplendent against the translucent white of the keeper bags. With no warning and only a few years of Japanese studies, he had done quite well. I made a point of telling a manager, and suggested that the manager write it up for his permanent record as an example of work "above and beyond."

In the evening, I played Kate Bush's *The Whole Story* on the overhead sound system. As it was playing "Cloudbusting," I helped a customer with a bag full of books and CDs find one more item, then walked with him to the registers. As I rang him up, he pulled a copy of the CD from the "Now Playing" bin. "Is this what's on now?" he asked. I nodded. He slapped it down on top of the stack that he was getting. "I was kind of liking it," he said, "but seeing that you were walking in time to the music told me I had to get it." I grinned, figuring that it was a compliment (though I certainly don't resemble any of the sleek and chiseled young men on the covers of the magazines and DVDs that he was getting).

Soul Searchin'

28 February 2004

One of the more evocative questions that I've had: Today, a woman came up to the information desk and asked "Where would your soul be?" I told her that the question had all sorts of possible poetic replies, but showed her to the R&B area.

A few weeks ago, someone asked me: "How would I find the blues?"

Deadpan, I told him, "When it's time, the blues find you."

Some Like It Hot

9 March 2004

The heat settings for the stores are apparently determined in the corporate Fortress of Solitude in the frigid Midwest. They seemed to figure that since it was just about freezing up there, we should all have our heat on full blast, despite its being t-shirt weather (as usual) at our store. Some customers complained that the chocolate truffles that we sell at the counter were slightly molten, but that just gave them a better excuse to consume their impulse buys immediately.

We had an unusual array of odd people, even by our wacky standards. One man came in dressed in a heavy coat, a hat, and a gauzy red summer dress that contrasted with his dense black beard. One manager seemed disoriented by a few of the other transvestites that had gathered, but I thought they looked pretty good. (On the other hand, they usually do: other than the ones who are completely messed up, they tend to dress and make themselves up well. After all, given all the trouble it seems to take to make the transformation at all, it's worth taking the extra bit of effort to look fabulous.)

I got to talking to a customer who was buying a DVD of a performance of Penderecki's music. We agreed that the composer's most interesting music was early in his career, and that he had gotten dismayingly conservative as he went on. Then the guy started talking about the supposedly terrible music scene in town, where he was unable to find a gig. He mentioned being an expert at oboe multiphonics, and did a few seconds of fluid non-linguistic vocals.

He said that he'd approached lots of the big names in town about doing music, but that they'd blown him off. As we talked, it became apparent why: he had nothing good to say about anyone, insisted on very particular parameters for his performances, and said that he required a large skilled ensemble with a full rehearsal schedule.

(I also was completely mystified when he made a series of complex repeating hand gestures in an attempt to demonstrate the relationship of his music to integral serialism.) I gradually came to realize that he had set himself up to never get anywhere close to being allowed to perform, and had blamed everyone else for him. Though I started out the conversation eager to help him, and offered to make some contacts (each of which he derided), I was glad, when he went away, that I hadn't given him my card.

The Four Questions

10 March 2004

In a recent post to his diary, Robert Fripp posted his four criteria for professional work:

- Can I learn from this?
- Is this serving a useful social aim (however we might understand that)?
- Can I earn a living doing this?
- Is this fun?

By these criteria (and by almost other, except the common chimera of possibilities for promotion, which are adequately addressed by the Peter Principle), I'm doing the right work right now.

The man with the purple coat and red dress was back today, listening loudly to hard rock on a listening station and avidly playing air guitar, the fabric of his coat swishing against itself as he strummed. Eventually, our plainclothes security guy escorted the man out of the store. He hadn't wanted to, but was given a direct order by a manager.

Despite his hard line to those who are actually causing trouble, the security guy is compassionate to those who are not bothering anybody (either through actions, noise, or smell) and are just in the store taking refuge from the street. As I left the store late at night, I saw the man in the red dress a few blocks away, slumped against the wall of pizzeria, murmuring requests for change, as were at least a dozen others on the four block walk from the store to the BART.

I had another instance of generation lag today, in talking to a new employee who was training at our registers. We got to discussing Van Halen, and I asked if he recalled the excitement that the release of their first album triggered. My brother and I, for example, had listened repeatedly to some tracks, trying to figure out whether some sounds were from the voice or guitar. Of course, he hadn't—the album came out some five years before he was born.

But I did manage to make good connections with customers today, finding them discs by, among many others, Lama Gyurme Das, Al Hibbler, Brad Mehldau, Mrs H H A Beach, and Split Enz. And since we're starting to get rid of our promo discs in preparation for our inventory in a few weeks, I grabbed a DVD by Nusrat Fateh Ali Khan, and CDs of Miroslav Vitous, Mandy Moore, a Charlie Parker remix project, and the double-disc original cast album of *Hair*. Wheee.

Blessed Assurance

14 March 2004

No one knows where Willis lives or how he supports himself. People have seen him at lots of film screenings (no one knows how he gets in) and at BART or Muni stations. For much of most days, though, he's at the store, crouching in the magazine area studying the film zines or standing at a listening station playing the same discs over and over.

He is silent when he reads downstairs. But when he's at the listening stations, what we're told is his Tourette's syndrome manifests itself in its full annoying glory. Wearing a static grin, he often drums with one finger on the CD bins, his other hand waving and chopping at the air in rhythm to the music, which he plays so loudly that we can often identify it as it blasts from his headphones. His grunts, hisses, barks, and spitting sounds punctuate his motions, maddening those of us who have been hearing him there for years and often frightening customers near him.

He wore his hair short when I started at the store, but now has shaved his head completely. For a while a few months ago, he had shaved a wide strip around each ear, as if he was modifying his look to better accommodate headphones.

When he comes out from under the phones, he often tries to engage us in conversation. He usually spins out from descriptions of movies he wants to make ("I got this great idea, never been done before. I just gotta find somebody to write it."), which tend to be slight variations on existing movies with magic tricks thrown in. Given enough time, he'll devolve into political rants, often fascist, racist, or antisemitic. (Occasionally he'll also shout epithets or throw his arms up in Nazi salutes when under the headphones. Those are the only times that we feel that we can intervene and get him to cut it out. We've been told that since his Tourette's is a medical condition, to constrain him otherwise would violate his civil rights.)

Then there are the times when, as closely as we can figure, he goes off his medication. Then he prowls through the store, growling, cursing, and muttering to himself and frequently slamming his fist into the walls. This happened on the night of the midnight release of the most recent Harry Potter novel. Having Willis careening through the store in ogre mode amidst a horde of sleep-deprived eight-year-olds was enough to make all of us jumpy.

We had a major performance this afternoon. A sixties icon was performing songs from her new album downstairs and signing it (and her other records, books, and posters) up on our floor. The space was packed with devoted fans from their teens to their eighties or so. As she performed, much of the audience seemed religiously blissed out.

I was in good form throughout the event, helping get the CDs set up effectively, efficiently ringing up the customers who were buying CDs for her to sign (awing many with my ability to strip a CD of its wrapping and that maddening top adhesive bar quickly and without tools) answering the many phone calls about the event.

One quest particularly maddened me: the computers insisted that we had no recording of Ravel's "Kaddish" for violin and piano, though I was sure that I had seen one in the bins. Perhaps my interest in Jewish music got the better of me, but I felt like finding that track was one of the most important projects in the world. Even though the customers had given up and were willing to leave without it, I kept ripping through the Violin section until I finally found a recording for them.

But there was a moment of beautiful clarity in the afternoon: when I was at the register, the singer passed with her entourage. Making eye contact, I nodded toward her. She smiled broadly and waved. And for an instant, I felt like a fairy godmother had tapped me with her wand and whispered that everything would be OK.

Caribbean Queen

15 March 2004

Early Sunday morning, not long after the store opened, a stunning woman appeared on our floor, looking for world music to bring with her on her flight to the Caribbean later that day. She was quite tall, with mid-length Blondie hair, a skin tight gold dress that left little to imagination, and matching gold heels on which she could just about balance. (Usually when I see women dressed like this at odd hours, I suspect that they are really drag queens, but if this one was, she should win an Oscar for costume design and special effects.)

As I flipped through the bins looking for a CD that she requested, she sidled up next to me, tilted back so that her back was resting against my arm, put her head on my shoulder, and whispered something. It was a difficult social moment.

Fortunately, I found the disc that she had requested right at that moment, and started talking about the CD and how it compared to another by the same artist. I also confirmed the location of my wallet and looked to see if she was trying to steal any CDs (though I couldn't imagine where she would have hidden them).

If that instant had had a caption, it might have been "Ma'am, I didn't quite follow what you're trying to involve me in, but I suspect that any such activities might make it hard to answer the phone at the same time."

Supper's Ready

16 Mar 2004

As Material Girl and I talk, she keeps busy by opening the cash register and neatening the money in it. We notice the way that we approach the money in the register.

Before I had started working in the store, I had trouble believing people in retail who told me that they considered the money in transactions to be utterly different from their own, as if it were, as many said, Monopoly money. We had discovered that it was true.

When I mention this to Material Girl, she holds up a stack of $100 bills that she had sorted and counted. "See this? It's more than my rent. But it doesn't feel real, like even the same kind of paper as the money we use." This is obviously good. But I wonder about how we got ourselves to think of it this way.

I worked late, since schedules got juggled in a staff crisis. One of the café workers got a phone call that a close friend had just killed herself. She tried to soldier on through her shift but broke down, and the rest of us shuffled about to cover, with Material Girl, who was supposed to close in music, dropping down to close the café. I stayed overtime to cover for her, until another café worker was located and everyone went back to where they originally were. When needed, we're all there for each other, limited only by the extent to which we know each other's tasks.

After I got off work, I came back to the café to get some dinner. (Necessary frugality over the next few days makes buying dinner there, using the merchandise card we get each month, a prudent measure, if not the most nutritious.)

Material Girl was working down there again. Since we often run out of bagels by the end of the day, I was pleased that we had several left. She looked at me and grinned: "You're tripping over bagels. You are such a Jew." I grinned back.

CHAPTER 5

She Who Laughs

17 March 2004

She Who Laughs is always laughing. Whether in flowing giggles, explosive howls, or the subtle glottal chirps that underlie many of her sentences, laughter is inseparable from her speech and inherent in her silences. I don't know that she is more consistently happy than the rest of us, but she keeps up the image. Concern and longing only rarely slip out from behind her facade of glee.

One day at lunch, she looked up at me from her celebrity fashion magazine and said quietly, "You know how it is when you're with someone, and when you're not with him, everything you see and think of makes you think of him even more? I want to have some guy think of me like that." She paused, then let loose with a quiet rolling chortle, as if it would reach back in time and make what she had said less serious.

Weeks later, again at lunch, she said without immediate context, "You know that thing about thinking about a guy that way? I think I may be there." But months later, she was again worrying about a guy to whom she had given her number at a party a couple of nights before and who hadn't called her.

She's about the same age as the average of our workers, about twenty years younger than me, but still seems very young (though she has mentioned to me how very young some of our other workers, who seem to me not to be very far from her in age, seem to her). She worries about her looks, her clothes, her weight, and the like.

Some time ago, she was wondering about the difference between the terms "gorgeous" and "lovely." What I didn't do, but wish I had, was point to a picture of one of the overly made up stars in her magazine, and say, "She is gorgeous. But you are lovely." With her creamy tan skin, large bright eyes, full lips, and ubiquitous smile, she immediately captures my attention, at least, when she enters a room.

Tenacious Tea

20 March 2004

It took a long time for the barista at Berkeley Espresso to search for the tea I wanted. The canister from the rack where customers pick their own teabags was empty, so he ducked down to look through the brown paper sacks of teabags for a refill.

By the time he had checked about a third of the sacks, I had spotted some alternative teas. By the time he had checked another third, I had decided that I really preferred another of the teas that I had spotted, rather than the one that I had requested in the first place.

I had trouble deciding whether to tell him that I had changed my mind. On the one hand, I wasn't going to benefit from his continued search. On the other, he had already gone through most of the bags. If he stopped now, there would be no information gained. If he completed the search, he would at least know for certain whether they had completely run out of the original tea.

I also knew that I get insanely tenacious doing customer searches at work. I get frustrated when a customer gives up if I haven't found a result quickly, and often continue the search after the customer has wandered off, determined to, at least, find the answer for myself. If I find the disc that the customer was looking for and he is still on the music floor, I sometimes trot over to him with the disc, which he may or may not then buy. I wondered if the barista had such a compulsive streak, or if he might be relieved if I gave up.

As I watched the barista work his way through the stacks, I decided that the appropriate course was to let him finish the search. If he would find the tea that I had originally requested, I would get that. If not, I would get the other tea that I had chosen. Had the shop been more crowded, I might have decided differently. But there was no line behind me, so no other customers were having to wait.

He completed the search and stood up empty handed, flipping the cabinet door shut with his foot. "No, we have no more of that."

"OK," I replied. "I'll get this one then." I popped open the canister of the second tea, retrieved the top teabag, and dropped it in the glass of hot water. The barista skidded the empty canister of the original tea along the counter behind him. It bounced off the far wall, teetered perilously near the edge, and came to rest against a toaster.

While I was writing the first draft of the previous paragraph, an ant made its way regally down the shaft of my pen, hopped off the point, and walked across the page and down onto the round orange table. I don't know how long it had waited on the pen before descending, or how it had gotten onto the pen in the first place.

Chapter 5

Each of us continued our work without intentionally disturbing the other.

Midday, a customer came in to our store looking for a particular recording of Beethoven's fifth piano concerto. We didn't have it, and couldn't order it in time. She said, however, that she'd be traveling through Austin, Plano, and New York City before heading home to Australia. I got her a brochure with the phone number of the relevant stores, and rattled off driving directions to the Austin and Plano stores and how to get to two of the NYC stores by subway.

When I told Rose about this, she asked me how one would drive to the store in Boca Raton. I didn't know, which relieved her. The thought that I might have the location of all our several hundred stores encoded in my head would have made me seem a little too much like Rainman.

I would never have thought before starting this job, that I would be any good at or enjoy be a (gasp) salesman. But I really get a kick out of it, and enjoying "upselling," which is what we call selling an additional, unexpected item to someone based on what they're already getting. My supervisor occasionally refers to me as "The Upseller," though others on the staff are also quite good at it.

On the other hand, I try not to sell anyone anything that I don't actually think they'll like (though I'm sometimes quite wrong on that —I've convinced several people to buy one album that I find breathtakingly lovely, only to learn later that they hated it when they listened to it; one found it "too poppy" which another found it "too classical"). I'll sometimes guide people to less expensive recordings if I think they'd be more appropriate.

Fortunately, we don't get any kind of commission on sales, so there's no personal financial benefit in selling things to people just to rack up the numbers. Besides, as one of my mentors in how to run a record store really well, MannyLunch from the Downtown Music Gallery, used to say, "I'd rather have you not get anything than think of this store as the place that you got the record that sucked."

That's one of the great things about the folks that I work with: we're all music and movie nuts who love turning people on to more movies and music. And, unlike in my previous jobs, I finally can explain to people what the heck it is that i do for a living.

(My multi-disk CD player just finished playing *Largo al Factotum: Famous Baritone Arias* and started spinning the banjo solo at the start of a Pete Seeger record. Ow. I'm not sure if I got whiplash or the bends.)

Time Passages

21 March 2004

We hit an interface weirdness at work today. Looking at the information on a particular CD, we saw that we had gotten forty copies in and sold one, leaving 37. As closely as we could figure, that should have come to 39. I told Rose that this was because we had to ritually sacrifice product to Moloch to stay in business. Out of every 20 CDs, one had to be thrown into a microwave.

Certainly the fires of hell seemed to be fueling our air conditioning system today. It was very hot upstairs, though yesterday some were complaining that it was too cold. (I don't feel cold as strongly as some others, perhaps due to having spent my formative years in Winnipeg.) It seems like Goldilocks is running our climate controls.

Partway through the day, I put on a CD by the heavy metal parody band (I hope they're an intentional parody!) The Darkness. As the overwrought falsetto of the lead singer started up, I heard what I thought was people in the distance imitating him. Looking more closely, however, I saw that two customers had brought in tiny dogs that had spotted each other and started yipping. Their sound clicked into the singer's pitch and rhythms to an uncanny degree.

In the morning, someone from New York City wanted to see if the branch of our store near her home could order a disc. I started to dial the NYC store, then stopped. "We can't call now: it's 11:15, which means it's only 8:15 AM there, and they're not open yet." Both Rose and the customer gave me a really odd look.

At that moment, the portable phone rang and Rose handed it to me to answer while she took over the other matter and proceeded to dial New York. It turned out, of course, that it was three hours later there, rather than earlier, and they were able to place the order without a hitch. Fortunately, they were both amused.

My sense of direction is notorious. It's not even consistently wrong, only about half the time, which makes it pretty much useless. And it affects a lot of arbitrarily binary things, like remembering whether clocks move forward or backward when the time zones change, and which is called Daylight Savings Time and which is Standard. I remember that Daylight Savings adds an hour of daylight to the day, but don't recall offhand whether that saved hour shows up in the morning or the evening. And I know that something is supposed to "spring forward and fall back," but can't remember without checking whether it's the clocks that move forward with respect to time, or the perceived time that shifts with respect to the clocks. Either way, my wristwatch is an hour fast right now, and has been since we last changed zones, since I haven't been able to figure out how to change it. But it will be right again in a few weeks.

What Is This Thing Called Love?

26 March 2004

Since She Who Laughs doesn't have a computer, I printed out the blog entry about her and gave it to her. She was taken aback, and charmed, though she said that she had disagreements with it.

We talked about our educations, and she was surprised to learn that, like her, I had never graduated college. When she referred to us as "autodidactic," I put my foot firmly in my mouth by saying, without much thinking first, that it wasn't a word that I would picture her using.

Since she has so carefully established the exterior persona of being giggly, brash, and fairly superficial, it can be hard to notice and remember that beneath it all she is quite intelligent, thoughtful, determined, gentle, and vulnerable. I'm rather fond of her, in an avuncular kind of way, but find myself tripping up as often as not. Still, we click in an odd way, perhaps just by tuning into each other's vulnerability and trying to be gentle in conversation.

Later that evening, several of us, sorting a stack of reshelves that included some romance novels, got to discussing the books through which we learned about love.

The Bird Lady said that she had read the novels in which women fell for apparently bad men who turned out to be "diamonds in the rough." In reality, she found out that when you dug down into the rough, all you found was, well, more rough.

Ms Broadway had read high society romances, and expected that, sometime during her teens, in The Season in which society functions occurred and romance flourished, she would be presented at a gala and be swept off her feet by someone princely. But the high society teen gala never happened.

I said that I had read the stories of the great operas, and expected that love consisted of people meeting in dramatic circumstances, falling madly and tragically for each other, being torn about by forces of history, and killing themselves three hours later.

Actually, more of my worldview was probably formed by science fiction. Mere mundane romantic quandaries paled next to the difficulty of loving someone who required a methane atmosphere, would burst into flame in the presence of water, would be crushed by Earth's gravity, or lived in another continuum entirely and could only be glimpsed within the event horizon of an all-consuming black hole.

That's Entertainment

27 March 2004

The day started off with a man who entered the floor slowly, waving about a short copper pipe with a round crystal at its end and holding another similar crystal in the same hand. As I approached, I heard him murmuring in what sounded like Arabic.

Apparently, this person had been booted from the store before for causing problems. When my boss spotted him, he called down to the Loss Prevention folks. "Do you see a middle-aged Asian guy with a scepter near the CDs? Keep an eye on him."

"Is he crazy?" the guard asked.

"He's carrying a scepter."

Eventually, while I was away or at lunch, the guy started whacking at the overhead track lights with his scepter. He was once again escorted from the store.

One customer, an elderly and fairly cranky woman, came in with a vague list to replace her old LPs. As I showed her the Paul Robeson CDs, she launched into a complex monologue about how she had a three inch thick FBI file just because she once attended a Robeson concert.

One of the things that she sought was a recording of Joan Sutherland and Marilyn Horne singing a particular duet from Bellini's

Norma. I had trouble finding it. While our imperfect databases showed that we had two collections on which the two singers sang and which contained that duet, I couldn't tell whether they specifically contained a recording of the duet by those two singers. When I told her, she said, "You have decided to do this just to be difficult."

She then looked for a recording of the Bruch Violin Concerto played by Gil Shaham. While we didn't have it in, we did have several other recordings of the piece. I recommended the Joshua Bell or Itzhak Perlman recordings to her, mentioning that my mother, a violin teacher, had said that they handled this type of material well. She decided to buy the Bell. "But if it's not good, I'm coming back for you and for your mother."

One particularly flaky man ranted in a wobbly loop of sentences about his own prowess as a jazz pianist, as shown by his being allowed to play at an event somehow connected to the previous mayor, and by his being allowed to play one of the pianos at a small church when services were not in session. He also rattled off endless lists of jazz musicians from New Jersey, which made me a bit abashed to be a fellow New Jerseyite.

When my boss rang the guy up, he gave him a one-time discount on the purchase, in apparent compensation for his having upset someone so much on his last visit that the usually unflappable employee had, he claimed, dumped some cold coffee on him. I would have been tempted to do the same, but even with our less than stellar coffee, it would have been a waste of resources.

And another customer held up the line while he explained very slowly that traditional jazz was dying in Britain, and that he was, shocking as it might seem to believe, the only person who could double on string bass and tuba in all of Newcastle.

After he got the initial purchase, he returned and bought two more items to get rid of pocket change before boarding the plane back to England. He paid for the $14.08 purchase with 52 quarters, 10 dimes, and eight pennies. (Yes, for some odd reason I remembered that amount, though I continually have to look up my own home phone number.)

CHAPTER 6

All You Zombies

28 March 2004

Another crazily busy day at work, about par for a Saturday. The parade of the strange had abated since yesterday, but we had an endless stream of customers.

At one point, I got stuck alone on the floor at the register, with seven people in line, people at my right trying to cut in and ask questions, someone downstairs repeatedly paging me, and the overhead music having ended. When Zombie Boy got back upstairs from having to change out the portable phone's battery (usually we'd call a manager to do that, but they were all tied up with even busier situations downstairs), I yelled, "Get over here! I'm drowning!"

Zombie Boy isn't really a zombie, and doesn't resemble one at all (except, perhaps, for the few moments when he has just come up from a particularly grueling café shift). But he's a big fan: he reads about them, writes about them, watches and makes movies about them, and wears t-shirts with zombie pictures and slogans. When I asked him how the new remake of *Dawn of the Dead* (which he'd already seen twice) was, he said: "Whether or not I thought it was good, I kinda had to like it."

In person, though, he's often frenetically energetic, bouncing from task to task around the store, putting happily aggressive music on the overhead system, and continually creating graphics. He starts off chance-determined images by blasting thermal paper from the cash register with the hair-dryer-like blower we use to re-wrap CDs, sketches phantasmic images of faces howling out of a smudged graphic fog, or makes strikingly realistic images of perfect flowers, using fine-point pencils and smearing shaved pencil lead on paper with fingers that quickly become so exquisitely filthy that they almost no longer appear to be fingers at all but some other apparatus of art, blunt yet minutely controlled. He's also made films, programmed software, done web design, and today asked me for advice on mixers that he could run his guitar and computer through for making music. And he's apparently running some sort of ongoing role playing game as well as classwork and other frenzied activity.

When we first met, several months ago, we soon discovered that we had been in the same place at the same time at least once: we had both seen David Bowie, Nine Inch Nails, and Prick in Dallas in 1994, when he was about ten and I was 35. He was living in the Midland/Odessa area (aka the middle of nowhere) in North Texas, and came in to Dallas to see shows by these big groups and others that flourished in the area at the same time, like the Toadies (later the Burden Brothers) and Tripping Daisy (which mutated radically into the Polyphonic Spree).

He has his own blog, where he posts his cataclysmic mood swings, in which I often see my own echoed in a younger, less extreme version. He questions his own actions frequently, worries about what may have been either past mistakes or valiantly difficult decisions, and wonders at the thoughts and emotions of others. And he hangs out with others of the music staff, and other members of the mostly younger workers.

As I left work today, he was fretting about the schedule which had him alone on the music floor for the last three hours of what should be a continually busy day. He'll survive, but I wouldn't be surprised to see scorch marks around the edges of his trademark black wool-like hat as his energy kicks into overdrive.

Few people on the floor today were quite as extreme as yesterday, but we did have our odd incidents.

Lots of people were looking for the most recent album from Anonymous 4, *American Angels*. It had been profiled on NPR this morning, and by midday all nine of our remaining copies had been snatched up.

Tom Waits was apparently in the store before I got there, which sent many of the workers into fits of excitement. Unfortunately, he never got to the music floor. If he had, even Rose, who is normally sedate, might have gone into schoolgirl hyperventilation.

Early on, I wandered back from the registers to the information desk to find Rose helping two women search for a CD. One spoke only what sounded like Chinese. The other spoke some English, and would speak for both after extended conversation with the other. We knew that they were looking for a CD of some sort of "Asian spiritual music" that had been nominated for a Grammy award. When I asked them if they knew anything else about the album, they conversed rapidly in their language. Listening, I thought I heard one of them say "Dalai Lama" in the midst of the conversation. I asked them if they were looking for an album that the Dalai Lama was on.

They and Rose looked at me in disbelief. "Yes, but how did you know that?" I told them that I heard the name pop out of what they said.

We still didn't have enough information to identify the CD, and they left without it (though I helped them with another search, which resulted in their buying a DVD of a performance of taiko drumming).

Later, Rose told me that she was quite thrown by my asking the question. She had been thinking "Please tell me that you don't also happen to speak Chinese but had never bothered to mention it to us."

I spent much of the morning running around, eagerly helping people (though one got annoyed when I asked her three times if I could help her find anything; she was sufficiently nondescript that I kept not recognizing her). A bit too much caffeine may have helped, along with the new greatest hits album by Guns N'Roses that Rose spun on the overhead system, which brought out my inner air guitarist.

When it came time for my break, I kept getting interrupted on the way to the elevator and doubling back to get things for customers. On about the third trip, Rose imperiously ordered me to stop working and go to lunch.

The other striking customers were less positively so. The man in the parka and red dress appeared again, playing air guitar and nearly pulling the headphones out of the wall as he leaped backward on some of the windmilling down-strokes. His hands, up to far up his forearms, were quite grimy, and Rose told me that he had lifted his dress to scratch himself several times before he was finally led away. I'm glad I wasn't there to see it. Rose was quite leery of touching any of the CDs or the headphones that he'd handled.

Everybody's Friend was hassling people in the café, not being confrontational but just engaging random people in pointless attempts at conversation. I heard him say to one barista who was studiously ignoring him, "I used to collect dead bugs. But I threw them out when they started to smell." He was impeccably dressed, as usual, with shiny shoes, perfectly pleated pants, and a white shirt that was just one step less formal than would be worn with a tuxedo.

He's one of the few customers whose email address I remember, since it's an easily remembered image from a well-known children's book, at a site devoted to that book's fans. I've seen him go on at length to customers unfortunate enough to sit next to him in the café about details of the book. I was amused to see one, some weeks ago, gradually raise his newspaper so that it completely blocked Everybody's Friend from his view. It didn't curb the monologue at all.

I had one moment of serious "Uh-oh" in the early afternoon. I had taken a ten minute break, and decided, rather than wait for the elevator to the basement to go to the employee restroom, to just use the customer men's room one floor down.

I had my coffee cup with me, an official employee cup with distinctive markings and a good lid. People were using the sinks, where I usually put the cup down, so I had to carry it with me into the stall. There weren't any level flat surfaces there, so I experimented with placing it in several precarious positions before finding that it would remain in place on the slightly sloping top of the toilet paper dispenser.

This worked well for a few moments, until someone went into the adjoining stall and slammed the door. The vibrations of the slam carried through to the side walls and the toilet paper dispenser, causing my coffee cup to slide smoothly off it it. The cup was caught, as if in a fireman's net, within the crotch of my pants. Had the lid been only a hair less secure, this could have led to catastrophe. As it was, the vessel maintained its structural integrity under attack, and only a few drops spilled. And those landed in such a way that by wearing the fairly long tail of my button-down shirt outside the pants rather than inside, I was able to hide the wet spots until they dried. Fortunately (I just checked again), they did not stain.

In a Land of Submarines

29 March 2004

It was a relatively quiet day at work, dampened by our exhaustion after yesterday's frenzy, the failure of the electrical power in much of the store for much of the morning, a lackluster author signing, and the large number of employees who seem to be suddenly and simultaneously suffering from colds or allergies.

The silliest thought of the morning was of a collaboration between Carl Sandburg and Carl Sagan: "The night comes in on billions and billions of little cat feet."

A customer complained about how much tax the city charged on the George Harrison CDs that he was buying. I told him that after what Harrison has sung about the Taxman, it was some sort of very specific bureaucratic revenge. He paused suddenly, the money halfway out of his wallet, and said, "Wow. Yeah, he did. Yeah," then grinned and paid.

In the afternoon, I saw a man, well dressed but in an anomalously floppy grey hat, standing in the classical aisle, holding an Arensky CD and staring blankly at his cell phone. I asked if I could help him find anything, and he said, dully, in a very precise British accent: "My doctor has just committed suicide." We stood for a moment, and I asked if I could help at all. "No," the man replied, "he's already dead." He sighed and flipped his phone closed. "And there goes my tax deduction."

Toward evening, two small girls, about six years old, came darting onto the floor and went running around the Rock and Pop section, occasionally squealing in frustration as they couldn't reach things. When I went over and asked if I could help them find anything, it took a few tries before, in fits of giggles, the smaller one was able to intelligibly pronounce the name "Christina Aguilera." I showed her where her CDs were, and dragged a footstool over for her to stand on so that she could reach the listening station.

(I was hesitant due to the raunchy nature of Aguilera's latest CD, but we only have clean versions in the listening stations.) Once she was up there with the headphones on, she stared at the CD and said, "Where's 'Lady Marmalade'?" That wasn't on the CD at all. I guided them to the soundtracks area, and showed them the *Moulin Rouge* album, with its prominent sticker announcing that track. She grabbed the CD and darted off to an older woman (her mother?) who was shopping for more CDs.

A few minutes later, I found myself absentmindedly humming the first few notes of "Yellow Submarine." When I stopped, I heard the sound continue quietly, in a high voice, near me. I looked down and across the aisle, and found the second girl singing the song. Our eyes met, and we shared a conspiratorial smile.

Gilligan auf Naxos

4 April 2004

I had my performance review at work today. I'm pleased with the comments, though, as I expected, there wasn't much of a raise due to the bump up across much of the staff not long ago, caused by the raise in the city's minimum wage. So now I'll be back up to earning about as much as I was 20 years ago. Which is, relatively, an improvement. I especially was pleased by one comment: a manager wrote that "every customer I've seen you assist has walked away with a smile."

Someone came to the registers today wearing a t-shirt with the logo of ARP synthesizers. I said that he must be a dedicated analog guy, and mentioned that I had played an ARP 2600 in college. He turned out to be even more dedicated than I thought—he rolled up his sleeve to reveal a tattoo of the logo from Moog. We waxed rhapsodic for a while about the 2600 and the old Realistic Micro-Moog.

The next customer also had analog circuitry on his shirt, which was from *2600* magazine. (That the ARP synthesizer and the magazine are both called 2600 is, I think, a coincidence. The magazine is named for an audio frequency that used to cause odd behaviors in telephone networks.) When I recognized the image, he was surprised that someone working in my job would know that stuff. He tried to baffle me by throwing TCP-IP (Internet Protocol) jargon at me, but I countered well enough to impress him.

I quickly threw together three displays at the store for our Classical Music Month promotion. (Cute slogan: they're promoting the "Buy 3, get a 4th free" campaign with the line "Create a Spring Quartet.") Focusing on the very few classical CDs of which we had 5 or more copies, I did one display focusing on the Naxos "A-Z" boxes, one featuring our own compilations of pieces by obvious composers and some of the new EMI "Great Artists of the Century" series, and one of other things, arranged in a sort of Tree of Life structure, with two of the San Francisco Symphony's Mahler recordings near the top. A customer, seeing it, said to his partner, "Look! A Michael Tilson Thomas shrine!" and bowed elaborately.

I had a funny bit of upselling yesterday. Someone was buying an album by a moderately well-known singer/songwriter (I forget whom). As I tend to do quite often, I raved to him about Vienna Teng's *Warm Strangers*. He didn't seem too interested. However, the woman behind him in line, who was buying completely unrelated music, said that she had to hear whoever it was about whom I was so enthusiastic. I guided her to the listening station where we had the Vienna Teng disc, and, after a few moment's listening, she bought it.

A friend in Austin once said that it seems that, while everything in everyone else's mind is linked by pictures, everything in mine is linked by sound. This can be a good thing. But midday yesterday, saying the sentence "I work upstairs from the Disney store" linked in my mind to the rhythmically identical line "Now sit right back and you'll hear a tale," and the theme from *Gilligan's Island* was stuck in my head for hours. (But some links must be visual or verbal—in looking at the previous sentence, the apostrophe in "Gilligan's" seemed wrong, until I realized that my mind had linked it to *Finnegans Wake*.)

The Manilow Mitzvah

13 April 2004

In conversation, She Who Laughs told me, "I feel sexy when I'm driving, even an automatic." To her surprise, I laughed, then, seeing her surprise, told her that I would try to ignore the Freudian implications of the stick shift. For all her attempts at a hard edge, there's something endearingly innocent about her. Maybe that's a facade, too, but I prefer to believe that it isn't.

Several kids asked for recommendations of rap CDs that didn't have Parental Advisory warnings on them. Those are becoming rarer than copies of *Kraftwerk Unplugged*. I may work with Material Girl (who is in charge of Rap, Hip-Hop, R&B, Gospel, and Blues) to come up with such a list. Come to think of it, I suspect that one exists out on the Web somewhere. But it's too late at night to go digging for it.

Tomorrow has an odd shape. I have an appointment near work from 11 AM to noon, but don't have to be at the store until 3 PM. At work, I may, as I threatened this evening, open up a copy of the new live Barry Manilow album and play it. I hear good things about it, and it focuses on his better, earlier material. (I remember a comedy album by Stevens and Grdnic in which a nerd character said something like, "I'm into Barry Manilow, but only the early stuff, before he went commercial.")

Barry Manilow did one of the coolest things I've ever seen when I saw him on Broadway in 1989. (OK, there goes all my avant-cred.) Partway through the show, he picked a little old lady out of the audience to sing "Can't Smile Without You" (admittedly, not one of his better songs) with him onstage. As they sang, the big video screen behind them showed them in close-up, with her kvelling over being up there.

At the end of the song, she started to head off stage, when Manilow asked her to hold on a minute. A man came onstage from the wings, and handed Manilow a VHS tape, which Manilow then ceremoniously handed to her: "Now you can prove to your friends that this really happened."

Telephone Tag

20 April 2004

As I got close to work today, I saw a girl outside the Disney store next door doing what looked like a complex dance with the bubble-blowing Stitch doll they had set up. She waited behind the doll until it had dipped its wand in the bubble fluid, then darted up and blew bubbles through it before the doll had a chance to blow them. She then ducked around to the front of the doll and tried to catch the bubbles on her outstretched tongue before ducking around to behind the doll again.

While I was at the register, two little girls began to play on the escalator that runs up to our floor. Each would run down several steps down it, stop, let it carry them back up, then run down again, giggling. Seeing them, I worried that they could get hurt, and headed over, running rapid scenarios in my head on how to react if one fell. Fortunately, as I got there, a woman came up the escalator, said "I told you not to do that!" and took each by the hand. I looked at them, then up at her, and smiled. She smiled back, ruefully, and rolled her eyes, then continued with the girls over to the children's DVDs.

A few minutes later, I spotted some boys of about the same age playing the same game. They saw me approach, and I told them to be careful. "We're not gonna get hurt," one sneered. "Yeah," the other spat. "We're not stupid." He dragged the word "stupid" out into a snarling whine, sounding a lot like Johnny Rotten, whose voice I doubt the boy had ever heard.

A well-dressed man stood in the far corner of the classical section this afternoon, appearing to be talking to himself. As I got closer to him, I saw that he was talking on his cellphone, with a thin cable leading to a tiny earpiece and microphone. I caught some of his side of the conversation as I sorted through the guitarists' CDs. From what I could piece together, his girlfriend had called him to break off their relationship, to his shock and surprise.

The conversation went on for a long time. While his voice never rose about a murmur, his hands gestured more and more expressively. Finally, his hands stopped abruptly in the midst of a motion, and he stared blankly at the hand holding the phone. After a long moment, he reached up to the phone with his other hand, stabbed at a button, and stared unseeingly into the distance. He then slowly reattached his phone to his belt, carefully set his face to a look that would say, "I'm in charge here and nothing's wrong," and strode resolutely to the elevator.

Turn and Face the Strange

27 April 2004

The store has made one small change in the placement of its information stations that I can feel, after a single day, is having a huge positive impact. Until now, the PCs had faced the inside of the information desk areas, which are built in the form of an interrupted circle. As of today, all but one of the systems at each information desk faces outward. This means that we no longer have to retreat within our fortresses to get information, but can just walk up to them and use them. When we're not using them, a screen saver kicks in that turns the PCs into the same search systems that we also provide in kiosks for customers to use. Not only does it take less time for us to get information and return, but with the customers able to see how we're searching, it makes the process more open and friendly. There is a problem with customers second-guessing our search methods and misunderstanding some of our shortcuts, but on the whole it's an improvement. Some customers have even joined in the search process, suggesting ways that might help us find things.

We had also had some confusion and effectively needless work caused over the weekend. Word had come down that a group of suits from one of the humongous media conglomerates would be coming through, accompanying a teen wannabe pop star that they want to pretend is a colossal hit. She's actually quite a good classical singer, but they want her to hit big in pop. We've been playing her disc a lot (I particularly like it), and customers react positively when they hear her one very good cover of a popular song from some decades back, but no one other than the workers has ever heard of her. Still, we had a half dozen huge posters of her album cover (which is also perhaps the least attractive photo of her in existence) and her CDs on display all over the place.

We had geared up for her to show up on Sunday, though no one knew when. I was given the combination to the store-wide overhead play system (the Music floor has an independent system), so that when the label representative phoned me to say that she was on her way, we could set her disc to playing throughout the store.

She and the suits never showed up. We remained at the ready all day, but there was no word and no appearance. We kept things ready today, today, just in case they'd somehow gotten delayed by a day. But by the time that I left, an hour and a half before closing, nothing had happened.

I tore myself away from work a little late tonight, my reluctance to leave aided by helping a late-arriving customer find a disk she'd like. Following her appreciation for some African artists, I sold her a disk by Ejigayehu Shibabaw, whose name I could neither remember, pronounce, nor spell, but which I found based on a vague recall of its location and cover image.

I tried to read on the BART platform, but had trouble focusing on anything. Gradually, though, I found my attention drawn to the sound of a beautiful voice. Partway around the round seating-stone from me, almost out of sight, a woman was slowly singing "Stop in the Name of Love," caressing the melody in a soulful, melismatic alto.

The song took a long time, and she stopped just as the BART system's mechanical voice announced the imminent arrival of my train. I stepped over toward her before I headed toward the train. "Excuse me, but it's not often that I hear someone singing on the subway platform quite as beautifully as you did, so... thank you for the singing." She looked up and said, "Thank you" with a broad smile, then looked down again.

Recalling the incident some hours later, I'm surprised to realize that I don't recall anything of what she looked like, though I have a clear image of the tattoo on the ankle of the woman who was seated next to her as I looked down at them.

Kid Howler

2 May 2004

Kid Howler would stand for hours at the listening stations, playing Broadway CDs and often singing along, loudly and badly off-key. I would frequently have to go over to her and remind her that we all could hear her singing. She would quiet down immediately, or often leave when we broke her absorption in the music.

The first few times that I had gone up to her, I had either come from behind or shifted quickly into her view. She would sometimes jump or shout when startled, looking frightened then angry. I discovered that I would have to come up to her gradually, starting a distance down the aisle then moving toward her slowly enough that I didn't appear suddenly. If her eyes were closed, I would call her name softly, repeatedly, as I got closer, until she opened her eyes and saw me.

Chapter 7

Her eyes were closed quite often, and frequently winced shut. Sometimes, unrelated to the music to which she was listening (so loud, much of the time, that we could hear it clearly from outside the headphones), she would suddenly throw her hands up to the sides of her head, wince tightly, and sing even louder.

She usually was alone. Though she was eleven when we first met and is now twelve, her mother insists that she has been old enough to shop on her own. Her mother would sometimes call the store trying to reach her, though if the girl was on a listening station she wouldn't hear them, and one of us would go up to her and let her know that she had a call. (This would usually be me, since the others tend to dislike and avoid her.)

The last few times that I saw her last year, she seemed to be experimenting with mascara. She had drawn fairly ragged black outlines around her eyes with it, as if she were doing so shakily and without a mirror. When I met her mother and grandmother, I saw that they had a similar approach, and wore it as badly. Talking with them all, I got the feeling that Kid Howler was the latest of several generations of unstable people, and that she might be as well off on the listening stations under our watch as she was at home.

When she was off the music floor, however, she was more of a problem. I'm told that she kept going to the erotica section of the book floors, hiding out there, and reading the books, apparently rather indiscriminately. When workers would find her there, they would take the books from her and shoo her away. Managers and security people had, on occasion, escorted her out of the store.

The last time that she was at the store last year, management called the police, suspecting that her parents leaving her there to read what she was reading might qualify as child abandonment, or some similar issue, and they certainly didn't want the store to come into any difficult legal situation over her presence and activities. She was banned from the store, and the security people were ordered not to let her in and to escort her out if she was there.

I recall that when I was her age, I used to go to the library alone quite frequently, and stop into stores along the way, greeted by the shopkeepers who seemed to know most of the children, even in that dense and increasingly dangerous city. But that was more than thirty years ago, and laws, customs, worries, and rumors have made the world seem, at least, to be a darker place and far less safe. As my bosses repeatedly remind us, we are not a library, and are a commercial enterprise rather than a public resource. But it seems to me that those lines used not to be drawn so strictly and so nervously before protecting oneself from lawsuits became the prime directive of our society.

Kid Howler was gone for many months, and I got to wondering what had happened to her. I wondered if she was still in town and safe, since I had a hunch that her home life wasn't the best.

I saw her at the store again on Saturday, accompanied by her mother. She came up to the register to buy something, which I don't recall her doing before. It took me a moment to recognize her. She wasn't wearing the mascara, and seemed a good four inches taller than when I had seen her last. But her straight brown hair, the white blouse that she often wore, and her demeanor were the same.

When I greeted her by name, her usual frozen glare melted into a shy smile as she recognized me. Her mother looked up at me suddenly, as if startled. "You know my daughter's name?"

I nodded. "She's gotten paged here quite often. And you and I have spoken a few times."

Her mother got a distant look, as if reloading the memory from a remote database. "Oh, yes!"

"I haven't seen you around for a while," I said.

"Well, you know she wasn't allowed in the store. I mean, she's twelve after all, and of age certainly to be in a bookstore, but they didn't think so."

"Maybe it's the peanut butter cup," Kid Howler said.

"The peanut butter cup?" I asked.

"She stole a peanut butter cup from a store when she was three," her mother said, nodding conclusively, then crossed her arms.

"How are you doing?" I asked the girl.

She opened her mouth for a long moment, appearing to be constructing an answer, her tongue poised against her jagged front teeth. But she just said, "OK," her smile fading again to a more guarded, distant look.

I rang up the transaction (a collection of Broadway hits on CD) and she handed me a well-worn twenty dollar bill. When I returned her change, she looked at the coins in her hand for several seconds, as if unfamiliar with them, then dropped them into a change purse that she put into a pocket.

Her mother said "Goodbye" as they left, and the girl glanced back toward me as they got on the escalator down to the next floor.

I saw her at the store again today, both times alone. Early in the day, she was sitting on the ground in the magazine aisle, holding a teen celebrity magazine but not reading it. Later, she came past me on the music floor as I returned from lunch. I greeted her by name again, and she smiled briefly then darted off to the escalator, looking back toward me again as she descended.

I don't know if Kid Howler has been officially let back into the store, or if the enormous turnover in our security staff meant that the people working the front door didn't recognize her. I'll ask the manager who banned her, if I see him tomorrow. But for now, she appears to be back with us, for better or worse, and some of us, at least, are pleased to see her return to the listening stations, safe for those moments and observed by people who care.

CHAPTER 8

Badge

7 May 2004

Sometimes things turn out better than you expect. Sometimes they turn out worse. And sometimes the amount by which they differ from your expectations feels more significant and more disorienting than whether the difference is positive or negative.

Just before 4 PM, my manager came up to the registers and said, "Once you're done with this customer, you're coming downstairs with me."

It took me a bit longer than expected to get down there, since as I was finishing up, another customer came up with a classical music question that another worker had pointed to me. Once I was done with that, I saw that my manager was already gone, and headed downstairs after him.

I tracked him down to the General Manager's office. When I got there, I saw that not only he and the General Manager but all of the managers then on duty were in the room. Uh oh.

My manager looked at me with his usual sullen face. (He usually either looks grim or is cracking up laughing, without much of a middle state.) "This is the most difficult part of the job," he intoned.

The General Manager asked, "Joe, what is the most important part of being a seller?"

"Knowing you're not an attic?" I wisecracked nervously.

"No, really," he said.

This was tricky. I had heard several statements by different people in different positions as to what was the most important part of my job. It was always, of course, the part that the speaker was trying to promote, including Loss Prevention, customer service, making sure things were on the shelves correctly, handling the money, or a variety of other possibilities. This time, I couldn't figure out what the agenda was, or which part of my job I was being confronted about.

"Um... helping people find the stuff they want, and... uh, suggesting to them stuff that they might enjoy that they don't yet know about based on what they want, and... um... ." I trailed off nervously.

"Making contact with the customers in the first place so that you can find out what they want?" the General Manager suggested.

"Um, right," I said.

"And you're just about the best person we have at greeting the customers and doing that," he said. "As you know, we've ended the Employee of the Month program, and replaced it with what we're calling the Best Seller award. And when we went to pick one, we decided that you are, hands down, the best seller we have. Congratulations."

"I... um... wow." That was unexpected, to say the least. They gave me a small gift card and a really dorky looking badge holder to wear that says "Best Seller" (from the design, it looks like it should say "Inpatient"), and will be writing this up in tomorrow's employee announcement printout. "You know that it might look like a pattern, since y'all gave me the first Employee of the Month award, too." (Yes, I say "y'all." My years in Texas showed me how useful it is to have a distinct second person plural pronoun.)

Some of the managers rolled their eyes. "Let us worry about that."

Lollipop Avalanche

8 May 2004

One weird chain of events today had me feeling like I'd fallen into a vat of thiotimoline: I kept getting requests for stuff that I'd happened to notice about an hour before I was asked.

It started when I was trying to find Herbie Hancock's *Empyrean Isles*. While our computers thought that we had several copies, I couldn't find them. I looked everywhere I could think of, including under "E" in case they had gotten filed under the title rather than the author. Unfortunately, the Hancock never turned up.

A while later, someone came in looking for Vietnamese music. I looked in our Asian music areas, but kept coming up with stuff that he found too traditional. We finally figured out that what he wanted was jazz by Vietnamese musicians. We didn't have anything we could search for as that, but I seemed to remember seeing something as I had been searching for the Hancock, and recalled the rough position and color of the CD. I quickly found, in "E" under jazz, an album by Peter Erskine with Nguyên Lê, which satisfied him.

As I came in from lunch a while later, I looked on the jazz display near the entrance for the Hancock, in hopes that it would be there. No dice again, but I did note a few things there. And about an hour after that, someone came in looking for a Coleman Hawkins CD that I remembered was there and retrieved.

The chains continued, including searches for an album of Tuvan vocals that I had noticed looking for the Vietnamese music, an album of Taiko drumming that had caught my eye while I was looking for the Tuvan singing, and a documentary on undersea explorations that was next to a DVD on the Tuvan singing that I tried to upsell to the person looking for the Tuvan CD.

My last transaction of the day was a mess, in a retrospectively funny Rube Goldberg kind of way. When I rang up the customer, the register paused for a long time waiting to print, only informing me after about a minute that it was out of paper. I loaded in a new roll, and pressed feed, but instead of feeding out a leader of blank paper, it tried again to print the credit card form that the customer had to sign. Rather than the appropriate information, the slip of paper had a few smears of ink and a blob of glue. I got flustered in trying to figure out how to handle a transaction where the form was ruined, and was about to call a manager, when the customer took the ruined slip, neatly wrote the amount and her name, then signed it. That seemed appropriate, so I took the form and handed her her credit card.

In handing her the card, however, my hand brushed a vase of lollipops that loomed menacingly over the register. The vase was quite light, and the lollipops were poorly suited to it, top-heavy candy atop long and flimsy stalks of plastic that flapped randomly over the edges of the vase. When our new café manager came up early in the day to refill the vase, I told her that with it sitting on a ledge overlooking the registers, it was doomed to fall over. She said not to worry. The worry was appropriate. When my hand bumped into it, it fell with a loud cracking sound and the whoosh of dozens of lollipops cascading over the counter, burying the customer's purchase and diving to the floor.

Rose, who turned around when she heard the sound, said that I had a really odd look of bemused doom on my face as I saw this happen. I stared at the catastrophe for a moment, then she, the customer, and I herded the lollipops back into the vase and placed it well out of the way, a process that took several minutes. I was fortunate that Zombie Boy arrived just then to take over the registers; had one more thing gone wrong, I would have probably been moved to leap onto the counter and begin laughing hysterically and flinging sheaves of vagrant lollipops at innocent passersby.

When I got down to the break room, I lit into the café manager uncharacteristically for having put the lollipops there. "But they have to be there!" she insisted. "Right at the register is where we get the best sales." Maybe they do sell best there, but the number of sales of 49 cent lollipops that it encourages was probably outweighed by the loss in sales of CDs and DVDs to the people who got fed up waiting in line while (on this and previous occasions) we had to recover from the avalanches.

While I was quite tired, I didn't feel like meandering home alone as usual, so I dropped back up to the music floor and asked Zombie Boy, who was getting off work an hour later, if he'd like to go get dinner together when he clocked out. He agreed, so I went to the café and got a smoothie to tide me over (supposedly "green apple," it looked like toothpaste and tasted like one of those odd flavors to which they apply the names of fruits rather than the fruit itself). I saw the café manager there and apologized for blowing up at her. She also apologized for the trouble with the lollipops, and promised to, at least, find a more stable vase. I then went back down to the breakroom, drank the smoothie, and fell asleep on the Big Comfy Red Couch until Zombie Boy appeared.

We wandered down to the basement of Macy's to nosh and thumb through a catalog of guitars, then hung out for a while in Union Square.

As we spoke, a couple came by, trailing tiny twin dogs in knit sweaters. The woman spotted me and said, "Joe! Hi!" I had no idea who she was. "This is Joe from the CD store," she said to the man. "He's the one who was so great at finding the music for me."

She then peered at Zombie Boy. "And you work at the store too. Isn't Joe good at this?"

Zombie Boy nodded. "Yeah, he's kind of my guru at finding music." The couple nodded and wandered off.

So I get an award one day and find out that I have unknown fans the next. Not a bad way to spend a weekend. We'll see how Sunday goes.

Bohemian Funky, the Ninja Diva, and the Peter Principle Declined

10 May 2004

It took me a long time to leave work today. As I did for a while yesterday, I fell victim to the siren call of the Big Red Comfy Couch in the breakroom and sat there while I attempted to gather my energies for the trip home. It had been a long and slow day on which I got a lot done.

The Eye brought a pair of sneakers from his locker and, landing on the couch beside me, removed his heavy shoes. (Or did he bring the shoes and remove his sneakers?) He stretched out his legs and rotated his feet in their dense grey wool socks. "Joe, massage my feet," he commanded.

I sneered and smiled simultaneously (which is a difficult task for anyone other than Billy Idol). "You know, I can never see anyone change his shoes without hearing in my mind the music from Mister Rogers."

The Eye nodded. "But I'm not wearing a cardigan."

(I remember, as a kid, seeing the show listed somewhere as "MIS-TEROGERS NEIGHBORHOOD," and getting the pronunciation of "MISTEROGERS" stuck in my head as one word with the accent on the second syllable, rhyming roughly with "Rick Derringer.")

We sat there and stared into space for a while. "I seem to have developed a severe case of inertia," I said.

"What's inertia?" She Who Laughs (or was it the Ninja Diva?) asked.

"It's how something that's at rest remains at rest, or something that's in motion remains in motion. Like when you're zooming around the floor and have to stop at the info desk, it's hard to get moving again."

"You know what word I love?" the Ninja Diva proclaimed: "Osmosis."

"What's that?" She Who Laughs asked.

"It's the diffusion of liquid across a semipermeable membrane," the Ninja Diva recited. (Or at least she recited something like that. That's from the dictionary.com definition. I do clearly recall that what she said included the word "semipermeable.")

"Or," I added, "it's the guy who parted the waters to lead us to the Emerald City."

She Who Laughs, as always, laughed. "Do you plan these things or just make them up?"

"Mostly I just make them up. Sometimes I write them down." I took my small notebook out of my shirt pocket. "I'm always writing phrases down to remind me of things later."

"Here, write these words down," she said. "Ready?"

I nodded.

"Bohemian funky," she stated.

"Bohemian funky? Why?" I asked as I wrote them in the notebook.

"I just wanted you to write them down. And I'd like to live in a place like that."

The Ninja Diva, who always looks impressive, looked especially striking today. Very tall, with short black hair like oddly but perfectly arrayed feathers, she mostly wore the black clothes that gave her the name, though today her look was accented by a red top.

She seemed quite daunting when we first met. She had a reputation for being hard to deal with as supervisor of the café, though she mellowed since then. She can also have a sharp and caustic sense of humor. She often appears stern, but has a warm and generous smile that can help melt the barriers.

She hails from Texas, as so many of the workers do (and others of us have lived there at some point in our travels). As we exchanged stories about our mothers and families in discussing Mother's Day today, I was struck by how different my family seems from so many about whom I hear. While I can be driven nuts by my mother's intensity and odd combination of precision and disorganization, and while I differ greatly from my brother's conventional suburban family life and my sister's avid orthodoxy, we've all turned out pretty well and relatively free of trouble. Hearing others' tales of drinking and physical fighting within their families, and the Ninja Diva's saga of her sister's troubles with the law and those inside and outside of it, I realize that we've had far fewer of many serious kinds of problems than many with whom I work. I had grown up thinking that our family was quite normal, and compared to others in my school and synagogue it appeared that we were. But by comparison with others, I see that despite our financial difficulties and the continual verbal stress among the grownups, our childhoods were strikingly calm, straight-laced, and safe.

Through the end of her shift today, the Ninja Diva was the supervisor of our café. As of Monday, she is again a bookseller, happier without the added responsibilities and not feeling much of a difference in pay. Our new café supervisor, the one in yesterday's lollipop fiasco, officially starts then. They've been working together for the past week or so, as she learns what's needed to run the area. The new one is almost frighteningly organized. Like me, she tends to compulsively document things, and already had made up some clear lists and forms to help the café run smoothly.

Unlike any other place that I've worked, there are many former managers and supervisors at the store who have returned to the ranks of book and music sellers. As far as I know, none of them have been demoted; all asked to return to the positions lower in the hierarchy. There seems to be a high awareness of the Peter Principle, in which people are promoted to their level of incompetence by having to take on tasks at higher levels that have nothing to do with what they're good at.

Most of us sell music and books because we love turning people onto them and helping them find the music and books they want and need. Our low pay helps guarantee this: anyone who doesn't really enjoy doing what we do leaves quickly to do other things at other companies with better pay.

I shudder when I contemplate what our supervisor has to do. In addition to helping people find music and movies, he has to run around the entire store answering calls from workers with problems, calm annoyed customers, shuffle endless paperwork, handle the counting and transfer of money from the register drawers, work long hours once a month trying to create merchandising displays based on the company's contradictory and inscrutable demands, improvise employee schedules on the fly, handle employee appraisals and discipline, and run around looking for product that hasn't yet gotten onto the shelves or has disappeared from them. I've been asked if I'd want to consider being supervisor if he ever would want to move on. I have no interest in it, since it would take me away from what I do well, which is interacting with customers and helping them find music.

Most managers seem to get into their positions from a simple mistaken assumption: the ability to do a job well actually does not suggest that the person would have the ability to manage other people doing the job. Management is its own field and requires very different skills. I've had the good fortune to work with some excellent managers, which has given me a less cynical view of the field than people often have of the standard Dilbert boss. The best ones have recognized that they were there to support the workers, rather than to be served by them. They would handle the bureaucratic juggling and buffer the workers from higher management and from stuff that would keep them from getting the work done. (As one boss once said, "I go to meetings so you don't have to.")

The best management team I ever had, back in the heady days of bountiful computer work (even before the dot.com days), was a triumvirate of managers who worked in parallel to run a team of about 40 writers. One handled the technical issues, one handled bureaucratic issues and dealing with higher management, and the third worked directly with the workers, supporting us in our work.

In that job, my title was "Software Toolbuilder." My official role was to write small computer programs that would help the writers get their work done. In reality, I spent only about ten percent of my time actually coding. Much of the rest of the time was spent wandering around, chatting, eavesdropping, and seeing what concerns the writers had. A few of these actually would need software solutions, and I would often figure this out and write the programs just before I was asked to do so. In many other cases, I found that there were other issues, from a loudly banging door that interrupted a writer's concentration to interpersonal struggles among the writers. At one point, walking down the aisles of cubes, I realized that each of the writers had confided in me which medications he or she was on. I helped some of them through some pretty serious crises (though dealing with all that emotion and stress from others helped trigger the worst mental/emotional crisis that I ever had).

And an important part of the job was taking these concerns to the manager who worked directly with the workers. She trusted me enough that I was able to tell her of things that were going on, while keeping in confidence the identities of the people who had complained to me, and to accept many of my recommendations on how to deal with them. When I had my own crisis, she carefully shuffled things so that I was able to get away to deal with it, and even helped me figure out who the key people in the company rumor mill were, so I could inject information on it to keep rumors about me and others from getting out of control. (I found that going to the rumormongers, telling them much of the truth, letting them know that we knew that they had the ears of the others, and explaining frankly the problems that might happen if delicate information was spread, helped keep the spread of information down. Many were quite pleased to have their position in the information flow recognized and honored.)

One thing that most stands out about this boss happened on an all-nighter that we pulled on a manic project. Late in the night, she saw that everyone's energy was flagging. She quietly ducked out of the office, headed over to a nearby supermarket then into the company kitchen, and distributed plates of green peppers and plain popcorn to each worker's desk to keep us going.

The team and office collapsed in a few years, mostly due to the boneheaded decision by higher management to base our entire business on a single client. This client was notorious for getting things going with contract firms then abruptly yanking the contracts and taking the work in-house. Everyone was left hanging. When it happened again, I made some contacts through my networking with other significant companies that could use our services, but our sales department proved utterly clueless in trying to figure out how to sell to companies other than our previous monolithic client. Everything fell over, and we were all laid off.

But our team's bosses were great. Two of the three had very little idea how to do the actual writing and editing that the team was doing, and wouldn't have been able to fill in well had we needed them to do so. But they excelled at the very particular skill of managing people, which was more valuable in a manager than the specific technical skill.

Many of the people at the store realize how different the skills are, and how being able to sell well has little to do with being able to manage teams (though, come to think of it, most of our managers actually are quite good book and music sellers). So we remain happy, if relatively poorly paid, continuing to do our work directly with customers and to serve them well. And serving the customers is, ultimately, what it's all about.

Looking for a Klugh

11 May 2004

My first customer at work insisted that we find her an album named *Purple Sage* by Earl Klugh. Annoyed that we showed no sign of the record ever existing, she stomped off to look through the jazz bins herself. A few minutes later, she returned, abashed, with the disc that she realized she had misremembered, Larry Carlton's *Sapphire Blue*.

Another customer was trying to find "the new album by the African people who did the record with Neil Simon." I knew immediately that she was looking for the disc by Paul Simon's collaborators, Ladysmith Black Mambazo. Once she realized that she had goofed, we joked about what they might have done with Neil Simon, imagining a play in which characters kvetched over breakfast as the choir circled them in the kitchen, voicing their thoughts as a Greek chorus.

Second Edition

12 May 2004

I was just listening to PiL's *Second Edition* a few days ago. It's one of the CDs I've been encouraging the young'uns at work to listen to (like Patti Smith's *Horses* and King Crimson's *Red*) since a lot of what came after is so clearly based on it. It sometimes makes me feel like the cliché of the old swingster trying to turn kids on to his music in bad 60s rock movies, but they actually seem more open to it.

The Masochism Tango

13 May 2004

When I went over to a woman in the Celtic music area to see if I could help her find anything (Compulsive Shopper Interaction at play), I saw that she was holding a copy of *An Evening Wasted with Tom Lehrer*, and gushed appreciatively about her choice. It turns out that she had just heard one of Lehrer's songs and flipped over it. I asked if she knew of his box set, *The Remains of Tom Lehrer*. She hadn't, and immediately bought it.

She said that she was going to go back to her hotel room and play the entire box straight through. "My daughter may hate it," she said, "but I'm going to make her listen to the whole thing!"

"It will probably end up like Stockholm Syndrome," I answered. "She'll become a big fan to avoid being driven insane."

Where Everyone Knows Your Name

14 May 2004

Partway through the day, a couple came rushing up to the music floor. Standing by the escalators and glancing around, they spotted my badge as I headed over to greet them. "You're Joe!" the man said. "You have to help us."

I think I said something coherent and witty like "Huh?"

The man took a folded piece of paper out of his pocket, unfolded it, and showed me some scribblings. "We were at this dance concert last night, and we wanted to get the music from it. The people there said that the best way to find music in this city was to go to your store and ask for Joe."

I trumped my initial repartee with a gallant "Um, wow."

While his information was sketchy, I was able to zero in on the music that he wanted. We didn't have it in, but I was able to order it for him.

Smile

15 May 2004

As we sat eating dinner tonight, Rose and I saw a man and boy ride past the window together on a single scooter. The boy stood in front, both feet on the platform and both hands on the steering bar. The man stood behind and bridged over him, one foot on the platform as the other foot propelled them, and his hands on either side of the boy's.

"Did you see the smile on that boy?" I asked.

"I saw," Rose said. "It's great to be a kid. We don't ever get to be that happy again."

"We don't?" I asked.

"Even when we're happy, we have the weight of all the adult worries on us." Her gesture signaled the years resting on her shoulders. "We don't get to forget them."

"I do, sometimes," I said, "when I'm writing, or when I'm doing music, and all that matters is the moment and the joy and the sound. And sometimes even when I'm thoroughly in the flow while selling."

It was another good day at the store. It was busy, as it always is on Saturdays, with a lot of customers, often with interesting requests.

I did one utterly bizarre bit of selling today, getting someone who was looking at a Swingle Singers CD to buy a Björk DVD. There was a train of some logic to this, odd as it may seem.

I had spotted the customer examining the Swingle Singers CD, and I spoke to him enthusiastically about it, telling him that we had done some of their arrangements in high school choir. He turned out to be a high school choir director, in with his choir from someplace in Southern California for a performance. He said that he was looking for interesting choral music for his students.

My first suggestion was the *Baltic Voices* CD with The Estonian Philharmonic Chamber Choir. He was already familiar with them, having heard them live and gotten both their recent CDs. I then recommended the new album by the Tahitian Choir, then *Vocalise* by Adiemus, which features a Finnish choir. Telling him about that, I thought of Björk, who worked with an Inuit choir on her latest CD and live DVDs. He immediately was interested in the DVD.

As we looked for that, I also told him about The Polyphonic Spree, who I described as "Up With People on acid." This clicked for him, but he decided to stick with the Björk. When I described it, though, a woman across the aisle said, "I have to get whatever it is you're talking about," so when I was done with the choir director I ran back to the rock CDs and brought back the Polyphonic Spree CD for the woman, who bought it.

(As I headed home, I worried that I might have sold him a DVD of Björk live at the Royal Albert Hall, rather than the one at the Royal Opera House that I intended, and didn't know if the Royal Albert Hall DVD would have the Inuit choir. But when I got home and checked, I discovered that no DVD exists of her performing at the Royal Albert Hall, so I'm pretty sure that I sold him the right one.)

When I told the General Manager about this later in the day, he dragged me over to my direct manager and had me tell the story again. Both agreed that that was one of the stranger chains of upselling they'd heard of, and probably something that few other than I could have pulled off. (A sudden moment of grammatical "I/me" terror ensues on contemplating that sentence.)

The General Manager was in a grumpy mood this morning—or so I'm told, since I was, as usual, tone deaf to these things. He led the morning meeting, but I found him hard to hear, even though I was standing near him and though we could hear the female managers well. When later I suggested that he project a bit more since he was having to compete with a pair of baritone escalators, he took it well, and said that he would. Rose was amazed. She said that if most people had told him that, he would have responded with a blast of attitude.

Clarity

16 May 2004

As is usual for a Sunday, the great majority of the early morning customers were either regulars or foreign tourists. I had been baffled as to why we got so many people from overseas on Sunday mornings until I figured it out a few weeks ago: Most locals would still be asleep, or doing more leisurely things than heading out to our store early on a Sunday. But the foreigners' body clocks would still be set to their distant time zones, meaning that they were raring to go at odd hours. And we are one of the few stores that is open before noon on Sundays anywhere near the prime hotels.

Once I started interacting with customers, I got into the flow of selling. Early on, I had the pleasing opportunity to try to convince two people to buy the latest CD by one of my favorite singers, Vienna Teng. The first, who had come in to get the latest by Sarah

Chapter 9

McLachlan, listened to the Teng album on a listening station, loved it and bought it. The other was surprised and pleased to hear me try to sell it to him based on his tastes. It turns out that he is a friend of hers. I did convince him to get the CD from another favorite band.

I had spoken to that band's leader at the store yesterday, and was afraid that I had made quite a faux pas. As we passed each other and she headed into the elevator, I had said that I had been listening to her album a lot lately, and had been struck by how simple her music was. She had an ambiguous look on her face as the door closed, and Rose called out to her, "he means that in a good way."

On the way to work, I wrote her a note, which I made sure would get to her, saying (more effectively than I could live—I'm better at writing prose than at speaking improvised social dialogue) that I admired the clarity of her work, how it never seemed to have too many notes or too many words. When I saw her again today, she said that she had actually understood what I had meant, and took it well. And she said that she appreciated what I had said in the note, since clarity is one of her most important goals in her work.

My weirdest customer interaction was at the register, late in the day. A man, close to blind and maneuvering with a cane, bought three sets of inexpensive DVD collections for a total price of $26.01. When he paid, and I gave him his CDs, he remained there. "Well?" he asked. "Are you going to give me my change?"

"There was no change, sir," I replied. "You had given me a twenty, a five, a one, and a penny, which added up exactly to $26.01."

"No. I had given you a dime."

"Sir, I'm quite sure that it was a penny."

"No. It was a dime. I never carry pennies."

"Never?"

"Never. I confuse them too easily for dimes."

Other than that, there was more energetic zooming around. Due to one bookseller leaving sick at midday and another calling in sick, they were shorthanded downstairs, and called workers down from upstairs to fill in. At the noon hour, one of our busiest, I was left alone on the music floor to handle all the customers. At one point, when I went up to a customer and asked my usual "Can I help you find anything?," two other customers answered at the same time.

At another, as one long-winded slow talker dragged me around the floor trying to communicate what he needed, I saw that yet another two customers were following us around trying to get a word in. When I finally figured out what he wanted, and headed to the computer near the register to look it up, with the two others continuing to follow me, a red-faced man barreled out of the elevator and demanded to make a return. I told him that the registers on our floor were closed, and he would have to make the return downstairs, he said that he had waited in line downstairs for "a damn long time" only to be told (erroneously) that the return could only be done at our registers. I finally called the floor manager and got her to send another person up to handle him as I ran around with the other customers.

At the end of the hour, I was supposed to go to lunch, but neither of the two other workers who were supposed to start work at that point were there yet. (According to another grumpy worker, who was near the time-clock in the breakroom in that hour, one finally showed up and clocked in at 22 minutes past the hour and the other at 35 minutes past, both apparently victims of the city's unreliable bus system.) Zombie Boy told me that he could handle things on his own, and that I should head on to lunch. However, the gauntlet of customers needing help never seemed to stop: it took me sixteen minutes from the time that I picked up my coffee cup and headed away from the information desk to finally escape into the elevator.

A few days ago, a customer passed me as I headed out the door at midday, and said, "So, you've finally torn yourself away to lunch."

I looked at her quizzically. "I heard your coworkers betting on how many times you'd miss the elevator by going to help customers when you were supposed to be on your way off the floor. You'd missed it twice already by the time I checked out."

Several times during the past few days, coworkers who have been griping to me about various things have paused to say, "But except for that, we really do have one of the greatest jobs in the world. We get to walk around and talk about music all day."

According to a list that I made while eating dinner, today I got to have enthusiastic conversations with people about (in no order other than how I recalled them) Adam Ant, Hilary Duff, Vienna Teng, Pink Floyd, Keith Jarrett, Pete Rugulo, the Delmark label, Jon Hassell, Loretta Lynn, Kris Kristofferson, King Crimson, Ferrucio Busoni, Edvard Grieg, Aerosmith, Weather Report, Damien Rice, Bill Frisell, Egberto Gismonti, Pat Metheny, Evan Parker, Aube, Eminem, Ofra Haza, George Jones, Tool, Phill Niblock, Nellie McKay, Astor Piazzolla, Enya, Alan Lomax, David Bowie, Buddy Guy, Mike Stern, Joyce Cooling, Christian McBride, the Crystal Method, Marilyn Horne, Tom Waits, Robert Ashley, Robbie Williams, Alanis Morissette, Joan Osbourne, and Winnie the Pooh. Not bad for a day's work. (And that list may make this page show up in a lot of odd Google searches.)

I was quite tired when I was done work, and once again hung out in the breakroom for a while before heading home. I spoke to my father on my cell phone as I walked to the BART then stood at the top of the BART steps.

Once off the phone, I realized that I was cold and wasn't wearing my coat, and that I had left work without it. I schlepped back up the hill to the store to get it, only to find that it wasn't in the breakroom. I assumed that I actually hadn't worn it to work and headed on home (where I discovered that I had, indeed, left it in the morning).

Besieged, Badgered, and Bespectacled

21 May 2004

As listening station howlers go, the guy in the Hawaiian aisle wasn't bad: while he tended to take longer to swoop up to a pitch than a rickety plane would take to accelerate to liftoff, he was pretty well in tune, with a pleasant tenor voice. What he was singing didn't seem to have many consonants, but I guessed that he was singing in Hawaiian, where consonants seem to be in short supply.

The people on either side of me trying to get my attention weren't as pleasant. While neither was being noisy, I wished that they might practice olfactory silence. The man on the right, graciously asking for an artist whose name I couldn't make out, seemed to have just arrived from a country that had not yet invented showers. The man on the left, like many of our customers, for reasons that escape me, reeked of Lysol.

By the time that I had convinced the customer on the phone that we did not have in stock the DVD of a movie that had not yet even opened in theaters, and that neither any of our branches nor any of our competitors would have it, much as it pained me to hear the child screaming in the background that he "want movie NOW!," the Lysol man had disappeared. I could tell without looking that the other man was still nearby, so I took a deep breath from another direction then turned to ask if I could help him. He asked again for the artist, "Lawyer Beesong." I ran through possibilities in my head, but didn't come up with a match. Probing for more information, I learned that he had worked with Bob Dylan (or, as he said, "Bobdy Lang") and did a song about a woman walking down the street. The tumblers clicked, and I breathed a sigh of relief (then turned away from him to inhale again), and retrieved a greatest hits collection by Roy Orbison.

Roy Orbison's name and music keep popping up. A couple of weeks ago, Zombie Boy had a hankering to listen to "Blue Bayou."

87

He only knew the Linda Ronstadt version he had grown up with, but I convinced him to give the Roy Orbison original a spin. He was quite impressed by Orbison's voice.

Then we had a flurry of people looking for CDs by The Traveling Wilburys. This was a supergroup from some years back, made up of Orbison, Tom Petty, George Harrison, and Bob Dylan, with producer Jeff Lynne. They did two quite enjoyable records in 1988 and 1990, both of which are completely out of print.

And today, we had the aforementioned sanitarily challenged customer, and the first customer of the day, a demanding woman with a voice that hinted at decades of cigarettes and breath to match. She had just gotten a car with a six-CD player, and came right to our store to fill it up. She was looking for discs by Edith Piaf, Nana Mouskouri, Charles Trenet, and Roy Orbison. As I searched, she carried on a non-stop monologue about various Piaf songs, interrupting herself to complain that the CDs that I found weren't right, then picking up the stories in mid-sentence, until I found all of them for her.

I got away from her to help a man who turned out to be looking for a magnifying glass. He had two Buddy Holly CDs, but the print was too small for him to tell what was on them. I rattled off the track listing quite efficiently, once I positioned each to best look at them through my frustrating bifocals. This is one area where my vocal training has come in handy: in the best K-Tel tradition, I can now recite the complete track listing of almost any album in a single breath.

The advent of the two smelly men came, of course, in a moment when we were understaffed. We should have had three people on the floor, but Rose had headed to the ladies' room, after getting permission from the floor manager. Yes, we have to get permission, since we have had instances when too many people have headed off simultaneously or been away for too long. Once she called and got permission, she paused, stared at the phone for a long moment, muttered, "... and this is my life at 37," and headed off. Immediately the phones rang with customer questions, and people suddenly showed up needing help, only to disappear when we again had enough people to help them.

The day usually goes like this. We rarely have a smooth flow of people coming in. They show up in clumps, though the groups of people aren't related. We'll have an empty floor, then a crowd, then emptiness again. From what I know of probability, some lumpiness in the flow is the usual way of things. Still, it seems to come about oddly. Maybe some week, if I get too bored, I'll figure out how to track the numbers of customers we get over time. Come to think of it, we could probably do that from the times of purchases at the registers, if the geek cabal in the Fortress of Solitude would let us at such data.

All in all, it was a mundane day of work. I did have some fun requests. A young girl was looking for an Emerson Lake and Palmer CD for her father's birthday, so I talked her through the ones that we had in stock and sold her *Brain Salad Surgery*, partially because she was fascinated by the "really freaky" cover. And a man apologized for asking for something he thought we'd never be able to find, an album he'd vaguely remembered was called *Switched On Bach*. I immediately dragged him over to the Wendy Carlos bin, sold him that and *Switched On Brandenburgs*, then added on some Steve Reich and Tangerine Dream before his wife stopped him as he tried to decide among Vangelis CDs.

CHAPTER 10

The Geometries of Illusion

09:26pm EDT, 23 May 2004

I can now further calibrate my reactions to alcohol: given two rum and cokes, I become moderately lit, appropriate to the circumstances. Add one bourbon on the rocks, and I lose my ability to find the BART.

I hadn't intended to drink much past the two rum and cokes. On the rare occasions that I do drink, I tend to do so efficiently, reaching an effective level of inebriation and then switching to seltzer and the like. But last night, the waitress unexpectedly handed me another drink, "sent by your friend."

A large group of us were celebrating the return of Jersey Girl to the city. She had spent several months in our ancestral homeland, toiling away in the city where my mother and her parents live. She

91

had finally broken free and gotten back here, enrolled in a culinary institute with dreams of opening a restaurant.

Many of the crowd that had been at our previous party for her were back. Zombie Boy, the Theoretical Kid, Material Girl, Rose, Ninja Diva, and several others that I haven't nicknamed yet were there, a party of about a dozen all-told.

Either being stranded in the cultural wilderness or returning to civilization had done wonders for Jersey Girl. She looked magnificent, as I told her the first time that I left the bar. And everyone there seemed to be in good spirits, amiable and relatively drama-free. The conversation was light. I didn't talk much during most of the party, content to stand around and observe things (which Jersey Girl called "very writerly.")

Ninja Diva proudly announced to us that she had become an "ambassador" for her favorite brand of bourbon. She apparently has quite a knowledge of and affinity for bourbon: she told me that "Bourbon" was her high school nickname, and that when she was a baby, her mother would sometimes include a spoonful of bourbon in her bottle to calm her down.

The ambassadorship has several benefits, few of which I remember. I do recall that she said that her name has been engraved on a new barrel of that bourbon, and when it is ready in ten years, they will contact her about some sort of special access to it.

I had never heard of the brand, and when I asked her what it was, she launched into a laudatory aria praising the drink. When, after she had stepped away, the waitress suddenly appeared with the drink for me, I was baffled as to what it was or who might have sent it. The others kidded me about having a secret admirer. When I took a sip and recognized it as something like whiskey, I guessed that it was from her. When she returned to the table with a mock-surprised, "Oh! Look! You have a bourbon!" I knew that it was from her. And, from my limited knowledge of the drink, it was indeed quite good.

I hung around until close to midnight, knowing that the last BART would leave the nearest station, Civic Center, at about 12:20. Rose had mentioned that she would be leaving before things broke up, and I thought that we might walk together through the rough neighborhood (though I suspect that people might be even less likely to mess with her than with me). As time wore on, though, she showed little sign of leaving. When I nudged her, she said that she would need a few more minutes. I had to leave, so I said my goodbyes and headed out.

While my sense of direction is always terrible, I at least knew that the neighborhood sloped in one direction (I think downward to the south), and that Market Street, where the BART ran, was downhill from the street with the bar. I headed to the nearest corner (Larkin Street, I think), looked to see the slope of the streets, and headed downhill.

Market Street was much farther away than I expected. The street is set at an angle to everything on this side of it, slicing into the neat grid and serving as the baseline for the unrelated grid on the other side. Up near work, it's three or four blocks from Geary Street to Market. Down near the bar (and I'm using "up" and "down" here completely arbitrarily), there are several more blocks in the way, including the Civic Center itself.

Once I got to Market Street, I headed toward Van Ness, remembering that the BART station was in that direction. My memory was wrong: the station, according to the BART map, was the other way, about a block and a half from where I goofed.

Van Ness Street was also farther away than I expected, and by the time that I got there and was certain that I had misplaced the station, it was well after the time that the last train would have left. The only thing that I could think of to do was to head back to the bar. Since the streets that I headed down were quite unsavory and I didn't like the idea of walking past some of those people twice, I took the better lit route of going up Van Ness and over on Geary.

Chapter 10

Due to the wonders of the Pythagorean Theorem, the trip up Van Ness was also quite long, and much of it was back uphill. But Larkin Street seemed nearer Van Ness than it had been on the way out, despite the map showing Van Ness and Larkin to be parallel. Somewhere, Euclid was either laughing or cursing.

By the time that I got back to the bar, most of the revelers had left. Zombie Boy was still there, as were Material Girl and Jersey Girl. The Theoretical Kid and the Dancing Guard, who had closed the store at midnight, had just arrived and were already well into their drinking. I came back and sat down quietly, and some (though not all) noticed that I had returned. Several of us discussed options for me to get home. Material Girl plotted out verbally a method using Muni trains and TransBay buses that was far too complicated for me to understand in my state of exhaustion and inebriation. Zombie Boy suggested something involving cabs that I also didn't quite get.

After a while longer, things broke up. The Theoretical Kid, Zombie Boy, the Dancing Guard, and I wandered off together. I suggested eating something, so we headed off to Tommy's Joynt, their favorite bar and eatery.

And at this point in writing, I realize that I've just written 1200 words about sitting in a bar, wandering away from it, and wandering back. And while some may still be reading, I realize that even I am not all that interested in the exhausting details of what went on. There was other stuff that I wanted to write about, and I'm not getting to it.

So suffice it to say that we went, we ate, we talked, we left. The Dancing Guard went off to his place, and the rest of us went to Zombie Boy's apartment nearby, where we watched *Fitzcarraldo* until each of us fell asleep. I spent the night there, getting up in time to head to work, opening the store in the morning.

CHAPTER 11

"There's Lenny Bruce in blue suede shoes..."

25 May 2004

Most customers drift quietly through the store, unnoticed by others, and engaging with us only when we approach them. Others have their tiny impacts, causing the occasional ripple of anecdotes as we discuss them in the breakroom then quickly forget them. And then there are the ones who rip through the store like a forest fire in Toontown, disrupting reality, confounding all in their path, and shattering decorum into flying shards of exploding fun-house mirrors before they zoom out into the night to become inevitable legends.

The call upstairs from Ninja Diva came at about 9:15 PM. "If something is listed as 'MU' in the search system, is it music? I'm looking for it down here in books and not seeing it."

The thing she was looking for was titled *The Trials of Lenny Bruce*, but she didn't have any further information. I looked at the listing, and it did indeed have that mysterious code. While all the codes in the system are supposedly documented somewhere, we can never find the listings when we need them. "Could it be an audiobook?" I asked.

"Nope, we checked there."

"How about a spoken word CD? I can check in spoken word and comedy." I headed over to the appropriate bins, bearing the in-store cellphone. "Well, nothing here named that, but I do see *Lenny Bruce Live at the Curran Theater*."

Ninja Diva repeated that to a customer. Over the phone, I could hear him bellow, "Thank you! You've been sent from heaven! And the other guy! Both of you!"

"OK," I said, "I'm at the info desk. Oh, and I just crosschecked *The Trials of Lenny Bruce* in the other system, and there's a picture of it. It's a book, all right, in the Humor section."

"OK," she said, and hung up.

As I looked up from the monitor, I saw a black-clad figure round the bend coming off the escalator and zoom towards me. A gaunt man in obviously expensive clothes, whose curly hair looked like a cartoon image of energies exploding from his head, he bore an armful of folders and papers as well as several books and other objects from the store. Fortunately, he somehow stopped his running before he got to the desk. If he hadn't, he would have slammed into it at about his waist, flipped, and sailed over it, making a mess of strewn CDs from either the Rap or Gospel bins, depending on his final trajectory.

"You're Joe!," he exclaimed. "You have the Lenny Bruce!" Those were statements, not questions, but both happened to be correct.

"Yeah," I said. "It's not *The Trials of Lenny Bruce* though, but something different."

"Great!," he said. He grabbed the disc from me and shoved it in the stack of his stuff without looking at it.

"Hey, while I'm up here, you do movies. Do you do movies? You do movies. Do you have the thing Dustin Hoffman did, doing the Lenny Bruce thing?"

"*Lenny*," I said. I looked it up in the search system. "It looks like we may have it in Drama."

I stepped around the desk and headed down the aisle to the DVD area. The man darted after me. "I need this Lenny Bruce stuff. I'm a lawyer. Did I tell you I'm a lawyer? I'm a lawyer. You know the stuff I'm doing." He rattled out some of the details on a very high-profile case for which he said he was the lead attorney. "I also do stand-up. Are there any good comedy clubs around here? I do stand-up comedy. I did some in LA. They love me."

As I reached the drama DVDs, Ninja Diva came up the stairs, brandishing the book. The customer grabbed it from her and hugged it to himself, then took the DVD from me. "Thank you! You are both heaven-sent! I fall at your feet!" He fell at our feet, his pile of papers and objects landing in a heap to his left as he lay on the floor. "This store is magical. I should buy this store."

Ninja Diva stepped away, then returned with a black mesh shopping bag, into which she helped him pile his belongings. The customer leaped back to his feet. "I've been to your stores back where I'm from in LA. I'm from LA. I lived there, but I have a place in Oakland now. Do you go to Oakland? I got a place near the Landing. Thirteen hundred dollars a month. Good, huh?"

"Better than I'm paying," Ninja Diva said. I didn't mention that I'm paying about a quarter of that, but I doubted that he would have been able to handle my space-challenged lifestyle either.

"You don't live in the city. Do you live in the city? Good, because I can tell you that I'm suing the city for five hundred million dollars on Friday." (Or did he only say one hundred million dollars? Looking for info online now, I see mention of the smaller figure, but I remember him saying the larger. But he spoke so quickly that anything that I understood him to say may have only been an approximation or even completely wrong.) "You look for me online.

97

Do you have computers? You look for me online. I'm in the papers, Washington Post, Chronicle, LA Times. This stuff is big."

"What's your name?" I asked.

"Hold on," he said. "I'll give you this." He reached into his pocket, pulled out a bunch of small pieces of paper, and flipped through it until he found two gray, fairly unprofessional looking business cards. "This is me. You look for me online. But the numbers on it are wrong. I've got a place in Oakland. I'll give you my cell number."

I read the card then put it in my pocket before he dug out his pen. I really didn't need the added information.

"I'm staying in that hotel down the street," he said. "And I didn't have any of the right clothes with me today, so I had to shop for clothes. I went into Macy's and only had six minutes to buy clothes. See this jacket? Twelve hundred dollars. These pants? Three hundred dollars. They do good stuff, good clothes, and can do it fast. They're sent from heaven over there, but not like you with the Lenny Bruce things. I could fall at your feet." Fortunately, this time he let the statement remain a metaphor.

"I got to meet your mayor this week," he said. "I was at a party, and all sorts of people were there, important people, people you know, and I saw the mayor there. And I went up to him and I shook his hand and I said, 'I've heard about all the stuff you're doing, and you're a great man, with the weddings and all that. I really respect you. But I'm the guy who's suing you for five hundred million dollars.' The mayor looked away, like 'Oh, crap,' and got away fast. But he's a good man. I'm suing him and no question I'm gonna win. But your store's good. You've got good people here." He raised his right hand and slapped each of us five. (Slap-fived each of us? No form of that feels grammatically correct.)

"So how much you think this store is worth?" he asked. "Maybe fifty million dollars? I think maybe I could buy this store." He pointed at me, "I'd have you run it," then at Ninja Diva, "and you'd be his assistant. You would earn six figures, yeah, six figures, and he'd earn seven figures, yeah, seven figures if the store makes a profit." I looked at Ninja Diva and smiled. We both knew that if such a ridiculous thing would happen, we would be much better off with her running things than me, since I have little managerial spine and the business sense of a mollusk.

"So I got a place in Oakland," he continued. "You ever get out to Oakland? I'm going to have a big party, a barbecue. You both gotta come. You off Saturdays? Sundays?"

"I'm off Wednesdays and Thursdays," Ninja Diva said.

"OK, it'll be on a Wednesday," he said.

"I'm off Thursdays and Fridays," I said.

"OK," he said. "It'll be on a Thursday. But right now I'm at the hotel down the street. I got a letter of apology from them. You gotta see this." He started to rummage through his bag for a folder.

Ninja Diva turned to me with a sort of trapped look. "I've got 373," she said.

"What?" the customer asked, looking up sharply.

"She has the portable phone for the book floor," I said. "So she may get called away."

"OK," he said. "You've got jobs to do. You do good work. You're sent from heaven. Here, you gotta see this."

He pulled out a slightly blurry printout of what looked like a legal letter. "So I'm at the hotel down the street. And you know how it is with treatment of Arab-Americans today. They see them, they call them things. You're Lebanese, they call you a terrorist. You're Palestinian, they call you a terrorist. And so there was this one guy, he works there, and he did some really good stuff for me, and I asked this other guy, big African-American guy, what the guy who helped me's name was, and he said, 'I dunno. Abdullah, maybe.' 'You sure it's Abdullah?' I said. 'I dunno, Abdullah, Abdullah, Abdullah, they're all Abdullah.' Now I know a lot of Arab-Americans, there's a lot of Arab-Americans, and a lot of them are Islamic and they may be Abdullah, and a lot of them are Christian, and they would hate being Abdullah, it's an insult to call them Abdullah.

And this guy's saying the guy's Abdullah, and I said, 'Are you sure? I want to write to the manager, tell him this guy's doing good stuff. You sure he's Abdullah? ' And the guy gets in my face—" The customer leaned forward till his nose was about an inch from mine. "—and he says, 'Yeah, they're Abdullah.' And this other guy comes over, also a big guy, African-American, and he says, 'Yeah, he's Abdullah, they're all Abdullah. Abdullah, Abdullah, Abdullah,' and I'm saying 'You're in big trouble here. I'm a civil liberties lawyer, you can find me online, you can read about me, Washington Post, Chronicle, LA Times, and this is a civil liberties disaster."

He backed off, waved the piece of paper, and poked at it repeatedly, "And so here's this letter that I wrote them, and there's all the Abdullah stuff in it, and I wrote the manager, told him I'm a civil liberties lawyer, I'm suing the city for five hundred million dollars."

To my relief, at that point another customer came up the escalator, headed around to the information desk, and looked sufficiently lost. "Excuse me," I said, "but I need to help this other customer." I headed off to the information desk, as the lawyer leaned closer to Ninja Diva, waved the piece of paper, and continued his story.

As I got to the desk, I picked up the phone there and started to dial it. Material Girl, who had been shifting the R&B CDs, looked over. "What's up?"

I pointed to the customer. "Saving Ninja Diva from an attention vampire, I hope."

"Needy customers. They can be the worst," Material Girl sighed.

I heard Ninja Diva's portable phone ring a half-dozen times or so before she was able to pause the customer and answer it. "Book department. How may I help you?" she answered.

"I'm giving you a chance to escape," I said.

"Thank you, sir. I'll see if we have that. Can you please hold for a moment?" She put the phone on hold and headed down the escalator toward the book floor. Unfortunately, the customer followed her, never pausing his monologue. I hung up the desk phone.

"What the hell was that?" Material Girl asked.

I repeated the tale of the customer in a greatly compressed form. "It was my duty to help Ninja Diva get away. I had a karmic debt to her for having bought me that very good bourbon on ice at the Castle."

"So that was her? We were kinda wondering who your admirer was. It was a really good party."

"Yeah, I said. I hope I didn't say anything too stupid."

"You? Stupid? What could you have said?"

"Well, I vaguely remember mentioning that the more I drank, the cuter the guy you were with got."

"Yeah, you did. And yeah, he did get cuter." She grinned.

I looked down at the clock on the phone and realized that I should have left several minutes earlier. I handed her the portable phone. "OK, I'm outa here. See you next time." I waved and headed off.

It only took me a few tries to get downstairs. On the way down the aisle, I was buttonholed first by customers looking for a Sigur Roś single, then by someone trying to finagle a copy of the *Return of the King* DVD several hours before it would be legally available, but finally managed to dodge the remaining gauntlet and, not wanting to remain exposed to further inquiries by having to wait for the elevator, took the escalators down.

Walking through the store, I realized that I was feeling incredibly energized. Somehow, I had caught some of the guy's manic fervor. It was sort of like a contact high (to which I'm amazingly susceptible). I bounced along, resisting the urge to sing loudly along with the music on the overhead system.

As I passed the second floor information desk, I saw Ninja Diva back at her post—and the same customer was still latched onto her, delivering his rapid-fire patter.

There were several people in the breakroom when I got down there. I started laughing as I clocked out. One worker looked up from behind her newspaper and cocked her head in curiosity.

"I just escaped the craziest customer. Ninja Diva's still stuck with him. He started by looking for Lenny Bruce things, then branched off into some really speedy ranting. He's hilarious, in tiny doses, though not necessarily in the ways that he thinks he is."

"Lenny Bruce," another worker said somberly. "A truly tragic case. A loss."

"Yeah," I said. "And I think this guy thinks he is Lenny Bruce. Except that Lenny Bruce would kick his butt."

I put on my jacket and hat, and caught the elevator back upstairs. On a hunch, I didn't get off on the ground floor, but continued up to the second floor. I looped past the information desk there again to see if Ninja Diva would require further rescuing. Fortunately, the customer was no longer there.

When I got back down to the ground floor and looked toward the registers, I saw the customer again. He had his purchases on the counter, and was directing his monologue at the bookseller there, Flash Impact, who gazed into the distance with a look of long-suffering bemusement as the customer waved his hands in the air.

I looked around for a manager, and saw the Guitar God perched at the ground floor information desk, impassively watching the spectacle. "That guy had Ninja Diva and me tied up forever earlier."

"Yeah, so I heard," he said. "We don't often get freaks who are this massively methed out." He sighed and hopped down. "So you wanna hear that new Dream Theater track I was telling you about?"

We headed down to the office, where I listened to some very good progressive rock on his MiniDisc player while talking with him and another manager. After a few minutes, I took the headphones off. "Sorry, I'm too wired to give this a serious listen. But I'll keep my ears open for it to listen again."

I trotted up the stairs and to the front door. The Twin was guarding the entrance. "Need a bag check?" he said. For security, the person at the front door, or a manager if there's no guard there, checks each of us to make sure we're not leaving with merchandise. If we have anything with us when we come in, each item is tagged, and the tags removed when we leave. Some find this demeaning and distrustful of employees. But, as the guy who gave us the Loss Prevention lecture when I trained explained, it also means that if anything turns up missing, the logs clear us of suspicion.

I opened my jacket like a flasher and twirled around. "I have nothing to declare but my genius," I quoted.

"Good line," the Twin said. "I'll have to remember it."

"It's Oscar Wilde," I told him.

Flash Impact wandered over from his register. "So, you got to deal with the speed lawyer?" I asked.

"Oh, man, you had him too?" he asked.

"Yeah, with all the stories."

"Did he tell you about the lawsuit? And his stand-up comedy? And meeting the mayor? And the bit with the Arab guy at the hotel?"

I nodded to all of them. "Did he fall on the ground when he was talking to you?"

Flash Impact shook his head. "Naw. But there isn't room over there to fall over effectively."

"I got his card," I said. "I'm gonna have to google for this guy." (I did when I got home, and corroborated the bits of his stories that I could check.)

He showed us another of the guy's cards, which had some further writing in pencil on the back. "Did he add you to his club?"

"Nope, I think I escaped that."

"Oh, man, that guy," the Twin said. "I had to go through that too. He beeped the gate when he headed out."

"Yeah, sorry," Flash Impact said. "I got so distracted by his stories that I forgot to run his stuff over the platters."

"I asked him for his receipt," the Twin said, "and he dug through all this stuff, pulled something out, looked at it funny, and said, 'Oh, wait, that's not it, that's a picture of my girlfriend.' Then he went into his rap while he dug the thing out."

Chapter 11

A nearby customer looked up. "You talking about the curly-haired guy with the stories?" she asked.

"You know him?" I asked back.

She rolled her eyes. "Oh, yeah, we all do. I work at the hotel down the street. He's staying there. He's had some kinda run-in with just about everyone there. Except me, so far. Guess I'm lucky."

"So you think he's real?"

The Guitar God came over. "That guy? Yeah, he's probably real. And a real loon."

"You know," Flash Impact said, "when he got to the reg, he reminded me of someone doing an impression of Dustin Hoffman doing Lenny Bruce. And then I saw he was getting all this Lenny Bruce stuff, and I thought 'Yup'."

"Yeah," I said, "he had Ninja Diva and me going nuts for Lenny Bruce stuff."

"He got her, too?" Flash Impact said.

I nodded. "He showed up at her desk, and she called me and —oh, hell, just read the blog tonight. It'll all be there."

I zipped up my jacket, waved to everyone and headed out the door. As I bounded down Powell Street, the looks on some of the people I passed made me realize that I was singing, somewhat loudly, what had popped into my head as a snippet from *The Lamb Lies Down on Broadway*:

> "There's Lenny Bruce in blue suede shoes
> smiling at the majorettes
> smoking Winston cigarettes.
> And as the song and dance begins,
> the children play at home with needles;
> needles and pins."

As I search now for the lyric, I realize that I had gotten it entirely wrong, and had confused Lenny Bruce with Howard Hughes. But I suspect that's the least of the confusion that Lenny Bruce would be implicated in tonight, and that he was probably looking down at us, cursing volubly and laughing.

CHAPTER 12

Laughs Last

27 May 2004

She Who Laughs is blessed—or perhaps plagued—with a disarming and often disorienting honesty. When I told her that I had posted a printout of yesterday's blog entry on the corkboard in the breakroom. she asked, "Do you mention me? I only want to read these things if you talk about me." I told her that it didn't, but Ninja Diva saw her read it later anyway, seeing her moods move from frustration to amusement as she figured out who the various pseudonymous folks were.

There's an episode of *Buffy*, "Earshot," in which Buffy briefly gets the ability to hear other people's thoughts. In one quite funny scene, the audience also hears the characters' thoughts before they speak. Most are completely unrelated, or the spoken words underplay the thoughts. But for one character, Cordelia, they are identical: we hear her think something, then she says it verbatim. These were in the character's early days, not far along the path from bratty cheerleader to benevolent seer that she finished on the spin-off, *Angel* (now also canceled, alas).

She Who Laughs is quite like that. And as such, some people have seen her as obnoxious or cruel. I suspect that many of us think the things that she says, yet most have developed social filters that keep us from saying them. Perhaps this is what I find so charming about her: whatever she says will probably be just what she thinks and feels, free from any sneaky agenda or ulterior motives.

I know others who appear to have this same kind of blunt honesty, but in them, cracks often show that reveal the supposed honesty to be just another layer of illusion. (A rule of thumb I mentioned before: never trust anyone who asks you to trust them.)

We often goof on She Who Laughs for reading celebrity magazines, yet she points out that we don't goof on others, such as the Bird Lady, who also read them. I think that might be because she will react so honestly and amusingly, where others might just grumble and close up. It's sometimes hard to resist the urge to needle her about things, and the needling can often become undeservedly cruel.

When I ask She Who Laughs how she's doing, if she's had a hard day she won't hide it. The laughter continues to flow, almost as punctuation and as a shield. She's told me, "If I laugh, people assume I'm happy. But I can have a bad day and still be laughing. It's just what I do." She's smarter than is immediately apparent, more literate, more astute, and more emotionally exposed. But much as a small animal might have developed an unexpectedly fearsome or disarming howl, she laughs, and puts a comforting veneer of apparent joy on things that might otherwise be too dark or painful to honestly withstand.

Shredder's Absence and the Fairies' Shadow Box

29 May 2004

As I waited for a bus after work, a man stalked up and down the curb in front of the bus stop. Dressed in shabby blue jeans with a matching shirt and jacket and a floral bandanna, he wore brilliant smeared lipstick and shakily drawn eyeliner (reminding me, though in only that way, of Kid Howler). Drags on an acrid cigarette interrupted his hoarse shouting: "You ever been to San Mateo? San Bruno? They got training camps there, man! The same people who did this right here did it in Czechoslovakia! The people you support: you stand in their streets, you ride their bus. Czechoslovakia!"

On the bus, as it lurched uphill on Haight Street, two men bumped into one another at one of the many sudden stops. As they looked up, one said, "Man, just for a moment there, I could see into your mind, and what I saw in that moment was beautiful." The other man nodded, said "Thank you," and returned to reading his magazine.

I got off the bus at Haight and Masonic. Looking for a place to eat, I spotted a place that Skyeisis had mentioned, though I didn't realize until I saw it that the phrase that she used was the name of a restaurant: Squat & Gobble. I had a passable crepe, the daily special, filled with perhaps too many ingredients.

I sat at a table alone, against a wall. There was another table in front of me, and in front of that, another wall with an odd box-like space, about two feet cubed, cut out from it and surrounded by a sort of frame.

As I ate, a man came into the restaurant with a girl who was three or four years old. While the man ordered, the girl darted away from him, ran around the restaurant, then perched on a chair at the table in front of me, frozen still and staring at the empty box. Her father, when done ordering, came and stood by her. After a long silence, she pointed at the box. "There's shadows! And shadows means there's fairies! And the fairies have wings!" She jumped down from the chair and ran around, her arms spread wide like wings, until her father caught up with her, scooped her up and carried her back to their table.

It was a crazy day at work, with everyone off-balance. We were short-handed to start with due to Memorial Day, and we had an unusual number of latenesses (including Rose showing up over an hour late), people going home sick, and not showing up at all.

One instance of the latter was especially worrying. Shredder, one of our part time employees, had been out drinking the previous night with the Theoretical Kid, Zombie Boy, Material Girl, and others. The group had all ended up at Zombie Boy's place, but had left at about 4 AM. After some adventures on the street, they split off in their different directions, with Shredder heading off solo back towards where they had barely avoided an altercation with a belligerent street person.

Shredder was supposed to be at work at 1 PM. He didn't show. There was no one home when management called his apartment. His sister came by some hours later to meet him, and was surprised not to find him, and disturbed by the story of his activities the previous night. He's usually pretty sensible and dependable, so this is unlike him. As she was told about what was happening, she asked several times if we were kidding. Assured that we weren't, she headed off, upset, to his place.

As of when I left at 5 PM, he hadn't been seen or heard from. I'm hoping he's surfaced since then, and will find out tomorrow, but meanwhile am concerned about what might have happened to him. I admit to being, to some extent, the Jewish Mother of the team, but what can one do with these kids nowadays? More as it develops.

The Customer Pounce

31 May 2004

One of my most annoying habits (other than snoring, but that only bugs roommates and the folks in the break room) is the Customer Pounce. When in the store, I'll far too frequently latch on to a customer and help with information or finding something when another worker is already helping him quite adequately. I often do have additional data that is useful, but it makes it seem like I question the competence of the other employee.

We have a directive to connect with any customer who is "within at least ten feet of you." (My perverse linguistic/mathematical brain wonders if this really means that we have to engage any customer whose distance from us is ten feet or more, rather than nearer than ten feet.) This means that we are continually talking to customers, many of whom just want to browse. I've seen a significant number of customers get annoyed when approached by multiple employees. I also see quite a few, when interrupted from the flow of their browsing, scurry away rather than continuing to shop.

And the worst case is when one of us approaches a customer more than once. I do this far too often. I have little memory for faces, and after looping around the floor for a few minutes will look at the people shopping and have no idea which I have approached already. There's probably some Jedi mind trick that will help with this, but I think the basic problem is that I have a very short short-term memory stack (though good long-term memory with bizarre indexing), and just plain lose track.

Yesterday, when I was on the floor alone and was dealing with a large number of customers, each of whom seemed to speak only a foreign language, all different, a customer came up to me and asked if I had forgotten about him. I looked at him kind of blankly, and he reminded me what he was looking for. Stuck without an excuse, I honestly told him that I had indeed gotten interrupted in the search and forgotten him, and quickly helped him look for what he wanted (some of which we had, and some of which we didn't). I think he actually appreciated being honestly told that I had forgotten, rather than a fabricated excuse (especially since I am incredibly incompetent at lying).

This morning was extremely busy but, as often happens on Sundays, things suddenly went quiet at about noon. I suspect that this is because we are the only store in the area that is open on Sunday mornings, and people hang out and shop at our store while waiting for the other stores.

I discovered that two of the customers that I see fairly frequently are father and daughter (or possibly grandfather and granddaughter). The girl has been one of our listening station regulars. She's about eleven, tall and thin with black hair and a pale face that reminds me of a Modigliani painting. She shows up after school in her Catholic school uniform, moving from station to station listening without expression. She always looks almost grim and deadpan. I have only ever seen her smile once, on a day that she showed up with friends, out of uniform, and I helped a friend find something. When this girl (whose name I haven't learned) smiled, I said that it was good to see her smile. She smiled more broadly for an instant, then the deadpan look returned.

I'd never heard her say a word, but Zombie Boy says that when he helped her and her older relative today with some DVDs of TV shows, she revealed an encyclopedic knowledge of early black and white TV comedies, including *Abbott and Costello* and *I Love Lucy*. From what I could tell, out of earshot, she appeared to be rattling off rapid bursts of information, deadpan as usual.

She didn't go to any of the listening stations today, and headed off downstairs soon after they looked at the DVDs. I ran across her sometime later coming around a corner near the periodicals. When I said, "Hello again," she almost smiled, as if Modigliani had done a trial sketch of the Mona Lisa.

As of when I left at 6 PM, no one had yet seen or heard from Shredder. He wasn't due in, since he only works on Friday and Saturday, but we remained concerned about how and where he was and what might have happened to him.

When some of us were talking about him in the breakroom, the Eye, who knows just about everyone in the store quite well, was baffled by having no idea who Shredder was, even after we described him in detail. It turns out that since the Eye works on Sunday through Thursday, they have probably never met.

Some Slow, Grey Bach

1 June 2004

The guy in the red dress was back today, though he wore baggy checked shorts instead of the dress under his parka. He did some of the most energetic air guitar that I've ever seen at his listening station. I let him be, though the Dancing Guard eventually escorted him from the building.

Willis was even noisier and more demonstrative than usual today, amusing several customers, though not frightening any this time.

One couple came up to the register after watching him for a while.

"That guy's crazy," the man said.

"Yes," I replied.

"You do retail, you get these," he said. "I work in a bike shop, and we get our share of crazies. There's this one guy, don't know his name, comes in just about every day, different disguise each time. Sometimes it's dark glasses and a wig. Yesterday he had a safari hat, camou' pants, and a pale shirt. And he always does the same thing: comes in, takes out stuff from his wallet, thumbs through everything, looks around, and leaves."

We had one of our more cryptic requests, from an insistent customer, yesterday. She was looking for a particular recording of Bach's *Brandenburg Concertos* that she had heard a while back. Unfortunately, all the information that she could recall was that the cover of the record was grey and that it was played more slowly than usual. We weren't able to pin it down, which frustrated me and annoyed her. Unless one were to have an encyclopedic knowledge of Bach album covers and tempi, I doubt anyone could have found it. But I did point her to a small local store that concentrates on classical music. If anyone would be able to help her, they would. I wonder if they'll end up sending their annoying customers to us in revenge.

A woman bought DVDs of *The Lover* and *A Man and a Woman* with a gift card today. "I just had a big fight with the guy who got me this card," she said, "so I decided to go out and just use it. We were trying to have, you know, a conversation, and it blew up and he got all judgmental. And when you start saying 'You do this because you're this kind of person', I'm just like— " She suddenly raised her hand to gesture "Stop," then rotated it at the wrist and formed a fist, like a conductor stopping an ensemble. That gesture surprised me. From her demeanor, I was expecting a crisp finger snap.

The custodians' daughter came up to our floor tonight. The mother and father both work for us, and the girl and her sister are around most evenings, usually tagging along with their mother.

Sometimes, like tonight, the girl helps out by doing some small tasks for her parents. Tonight she showed up dragging a large plastic bag behind her into which she emptied the wastebaskets. I tried to help her by holding the bag open as she dumped one of the large baskets. "Don't do that," she commanded. "The inside of the bag will get your hands dirty."

As she emptied the wastebasket she said, unprompted. "I like working. I like doing things to make people happy."

"Me, too," I said. "That's why I like this job. People are happy when they get music."

The girl will be turning nine on Thursday, and told me that she was worried that no one would remember her birthday. I told a few other workers. Maybe some who work on Thursday (I'm off that day) will remember to wish her a happy birthday. I may put a note up on the bulletin board at work tomorrow.

Marley's Third

3 June 2004

Material Girl wasn't feeling well at work yesterday. Apparently something she had eaten had disagreed with her, and she was variably queasy from the time that she came in until the time that I left.

Blessed with a mild Long Island accent and a New Yorker's affinity for the large gesture, her voice carries well around the room. She also swears like the proverbial sailor (though, knowing few sailors, I don't know first hand how or to what extent they actually swear). She seems to have few filters and little fear. Inspired by the moment, she says what she wants to say, regardless of who is within earshot.

Soon after she arrived at the information desk in the afternoon, she announced, "I'm feeling kinda nauseous." Halfway across the floor, the customer that I was helping looked over at her and said quietly in a dry British accent, "Thank you for sharing that. Would you like to use my backpack?"

We had an unusually high number of British accents in the air yesterday, even greater than the large amount of British customers that we usually get. Several commented on our good prices. CDs are so expensive over there that imported British CDs are often cheaper here than at home.

Chapter 12

I found one group of customers particularly annoying. Faced with disappointments, such as our inability to play them any CD that they want (our scan and play system is due in two months—though it's been due in two months for the past six months or so), they frown slightly and murmur "Hmm. Pity.," and continue to stand and stare at us as if that will fix the problem. They seem to be counting on us to come up with a better solution, but we often don't have one. And when we loop back to explain things again, they repeat the murmur of "Pity" and don't move. The only hope is for us to be called away by another customer. Even then, though, the murmuring ones tend to remain where they were, watching us, as if we might have a bright idea and return with a solution.

I start to feel class issues rising quite strongly when this happens. I also feel this when dealing with some American customers, usually men in their mid-20s, either perfectly dressed or wearing ostentatiously sloppy clothes that appear carefully selected to indicate that they are above having to deal with the norms within which the rest of us live. The perfectly dressed ones tend also to be very fit, where as the others are often quite overweight. But the behavior of each is the same, a condescending exaggeratedly simple talk as if we are in our jobs because of low IQs or other problems.

I'll admit that in years past I had a fairly low estimation of people doing my current job. After all, I was earning big money, working long hours with high powered people who were convinced that we were changing the world in ways that mere clerks probably couldn't understand. I had no idea how anyone could find selling things at a retail level at all fulfilling (though I made an exception for people who owned and ran very cool stores).

But nowadays I get a lot more fulfillment selling music to people, even if I can't convince myself that I'm changing the world on some sort of macrocosmic level. For that matter, the idea of people selling these round objects in rectangular boxes is probably on the way out. I suspect that things will be evolving more toward the downloading of tracks, If people come into anything like a current CD store at all, it will be to burn CDs one at a time in special kiosks. (On the other hand, there may still be a small market for prefab discs that would be kept in stock for quick impulse buys.)

My hunch is that those of us who survive in the business will be the ones who will be most able to help people find music that they want, based on intuitive analyses of their desires and the ability to figure out what they want based on fuzzy information. The biggest reason to come into a store would be to check with knowledgeable people who could connect you with the good music. Otherwise, you could probably do just about everything from home.

On the other hand, this could be an utterly self-serving delusion to convince myself that I'd survive. After all, in the bizarro world of the dot.com economy, everyone knew that the bubble couldn't last, but each of us had a narrative to explain why his own niche in the industry would survive. We coasted along somewhat haughtily, sure that we'd continue making the big money based more on chutzpah than any particular skill.

So when I deal with the condescending nouveaux riche, I have to avoid the temptation to give them the dead-eye glare and announce "You know, I used to be you. And someday, you're going to be me." (Though last December, after one particular arrogant idiot departed late in the evening, leaving only employees on the floor, I did walk dramatically to the escalator, and, once sure he was out of earshot, point my finger down the stairs and bellow, "I am the Ghost of Christmas Yet to Come.")

One of these, who had been among the most annoying, comes in at least once a week, a nearly spherical American man with long dark hair, usually wearing shorts and sandals. Any attempt to communicate with him is met with an overly gentle whisper, as if he were calming an overwrought toddler or puppy. Many of us just won't talk to him anymore, other than the bare minimum needed for transactions. If he ever wants help, he can ask for it—but I doubted that he would ever think that we lower beings could ever help him.

But tonight, after several years of our putting up with him, he sidled over to me as I was shelving some DVDs. He was carrying several packages, not the usual anime and science fiction action-adventure that he tends to get, but romantic comedies, love stories, and other things usually considered as "chick flicks."

"Have you seen any of these? Which of these do you, uh, think a girl would, um, like?"

I looked over and up at him, and, Spock-like, raised a single eyebrow.

"I'm, uh, there's, uh, this girl, and we've, well, I've, you know, and she might, uh, well, so, which should I, uh, get her?"

"Hmm." I took the discs from him and flipped through them. "What movies do you know that she likes?"

He looked at the discs, then off into the vague distance, then back down. "I don't, um, well, she's in my, uh, class, and we're doing animation, and she, well, she watches some of the same animation that, uh, I do."

"Well, then, I think you should get her something like the stuff you both watch." I looked at the spine of the discs that he had selected. "Has she mentioned liking these?"

"No, but she, um, well, yeah, she's a girl, so I thought. . . "

"I think you should go with something more like what you both like, rather than trying to jump into a whole other genre. Can I guess that she's already seen everything available by Miyazaki?"

"I don't know. but, yeah, that might be, well. yeah." He took the stack of discs back from me and headed toward the anime, then turned back to me.

"In your, um, well, with girls, like, um, if she likes it, what should I, um, well, what do I do next?"

"I can recommend DVDs for you," I said, then sighed. "But asking me for romantic advice is like asking Stevie Wonder for advice on driving."

One of the British voices (Remember the British voices, a few thousand paragraphs ago?) yesterday particularly stood out. A tiny blond girl showed up in the evening with her family. While they looked quietly through the discs, she kept darting over to the children's DVDs, pulling them off the shelves and bringing them to her father. She continually called "Daddy!" in an exact accent, crisp as a finger snap. The "D" sounds in "Daddy" were partially voiced and partially unvoiced. When I heard them from close up, a quiet clicking sound accompanied each of them.

I got lunch yesterday at the Theater II deli around the corner from the store. The woman in line behind me announced her order as "Hamas with two pitas?"

The woman behind the corner stopped cold in the midst of putting my falafel together. "What?" she asked.

The customer repeated her order, "Hamas with two pitas."

They stared at each other for a long moment before I interjected, "I think she means 'hummus'."

"Yes, hummus, sorry," the customer said. They both relaxed.

When the customer had left, I said, "For a moment, I thought that was a political comment, not a lunch order."

"Yes," the sandwich maker said. "Here we maybe have jihad sometimes, but definitely no Hamas."

As I returned from lunch, a man in a bright yellow sweatshirt stopped in front of the store. He pointed into the air, announced "Bookstore! Four floors!" to no one in particular, then walked on.

A customer handed me a note that she had written indicating the music that she was looking for: "Broke Music by Anthony O. Vivotte." Fortunately, a few questions determined that she was looking for baroque music by Antonio Vivaldi. We actually had some of the music on a listening station that was not yet broken, and was able to confirm that this was what she wanted.

At the time that I left the store in the evening, there were four people on the music floor, all scruffy. I warned the Guitar God that one of them was ranting belligerently at someone we couldn't see. He shrugged. "Call me if he talks to a real person."

Chapter 12

In the half hour before I left, I asked Material Girl if she could cover the information desk, since I had to do some work putting CDs into cabinets. (Based on seeing some patterns of theft develop in the store, I decided, to my disappointment, that we really did have to keep a certain set of CDs locked up.) She looked up from a music magazine and said, "You always have stuff to do. You always have all these projects. But maybe that's why they keep making you Employee of the Month and stuff." Well, yeah.

CHAPTER 13

Real People

5 June 2004

The inside of the store is just dark enough, compared with the morning sun, that as we stand outside and wait to be let in for the opening shift, the window glass acts as a translucent mirror. We have trouble distinguishing the reflections of people across the street from the real people deep in the store until they either step around the book displays or pass like ghosts right through them. We can be quite sure that the ethereal cable cars and SUVs that we see pass through the store are really behind us. But it can be disorienting when the ghost next to your own reflection appears to say hello, a real coworker having quietly stepped up to wait alongside and slightly in back of you for someone to unlock the doors.

Chapter 13

The day was weirdly quiet for a Saturday, with no mad crushes of customers. Little happened of any note. There was just enough of a flow of people that I was able to get little done in my section, but I may get to do more Sunday.

I find myself continually annoyed when customers are looking for a particular item, but ask where we have a category in which they think it might fall, such as Anime Soundtracks, Classic DVDs, Pop Vocals, or Electronic Music. I recognize that any taxonomy of music or film is pretty arbitrary, but they come in with a categorization in their heads, look for a sign with that category, and, not seeing it, assume that we don't have that kind of item. Whenever a customer asks me about a category that we don't have—and often when they ask about one that we do—I immediately ask if they are looking for a specific artist. They usually are, but, curiously, are reluctant to reveal who it is.

Shredder is alive and well, and both amused and miffed to have become the subject of local legend. Since he returned to work on Thursday, people have been telling back to him stories of his having spent a night in jail after winning a brawl with a belligerent street person.

The reality turns out, as usual, to be more mundane: after several days of little-to-no sleep, including finishing up papers for school, taking finals, and working, he had indeed, against his better judgment, gone drinking with the coworkers. (That sentence needed far too many commas.) After the group left Zombie Boy's apartment, he had split off and gone straight home, a few blocks away. He had then crashed hard, sleeping through his alarm, which was still ringing when he awoke several hours after he was supposed to be at work. He had called in and told a manager, but word hadn't made it to the workers.

Touch of Grey

8 June 2004

The Southpaw isn't really a southpaw, though he is from the south (North Carolina, I believe). But the name stuck in my head when wondering what to call him in the blog, and he liked it when I mentioned it to him. He doesn't have what I would hear as a southern accent (unless he wants to), but rather has a general Midwestern voice. And he has the warmest laugh I have ever heard from anyone. He's one of the few people that I feel that I would trust completely; if I were to choose with which of the people on the staff I would have to be stuck on the proverbial desert island, he would be the one. He'd be good company and is endlessly resourceful.

He's been at the store longer than almost anyone else on the music staff. He's one of several former managers who has moved back down to a non-managerial level, having been the head of training as well as having held other positions. He's also one of the older members of the staff: I think he, Rose, and The Pippick are all about the same age, seven or eight years younger than me. I would have guessed him as younger, except for the small bits of grey hair near his ears.

(As far as I can tell, everyone older than me there has grey hair, and one who turns out to be a tad younger is completely grey. People tend to read me as a good decade younger than I am. One customer tonight, asking about Nik Kershaw, said that I would be too young to remember him, since he had his hits in the late 70s.)

He does seem more mature than many of the rest, even those his own age. He manages to stay apart from and disdain much of the drama surrounding the team, and doesn't care much for those who eagerly participate in it.

He mentioned today (or was it yesterday?) that he tends to be wary of and initially dislike new people when they come on board. "My first take is not to like people, but then I usually warm up to them over time. There are a few who I started out not liking and still don't."

"What did you think of me?" I asked. "I figure that when I popped in out of nowhere and took over classical, you must have been like 'who the hell is this guy?' "

"Yeah, at first I wasn't sure about how you seemed to know all this stuff and I felt kind of threatened by the know-it-all angle. But now I know that you do know it, and I kind of like it."

I did what may have been my strangest bit of upselling tonight. I had helped a couple from Canada find some Johnny Cash CDs, and was ringing them up at the register. Looking at the woman's credit card, I saw that her first name was Savitri. I mentioned to her that I had been in a version of an opera of that name. (A very loose version: two singers who had been in a conventional production of the piece sang their parts as I improvised on violin.) They hadn't heard of it, and the husband seemed not to know about the derivation of the name. The wife recounted the story as told by Sri Aurobindo. I dashed over to the Gustav Holst bin, found a disc with the chamber opera, and the husband bought it.

A few minutes later, I convinced a man who was buying a book on John Coltrane to also buy a much better book on him by Lewis Porter. He was also buying a CD of Eric Dolphy.

"I was fortunate to see Eric Dolphy perform since many years ago," he told me. "1964, I think it was. He was performing in Sweden with Charles Mingus. They had been supposed to have a trumpet player, but he became ill in England, so they were performing without him. The arrangements all involved the trumpet, and the pieces did not work well without him, and the musicians looked unhappy. Then Charles Mingus looked to the offstage and saw that a man was running a tape recorder, recording the performance without having permission to record. Charles Mingus put down his bass and walked off the stage to the man, where I could still see him past the curtain. He said nothing, and picked up the tape recorder over his head and smashed it to the ground. Then he again said nothing, but walked back on stage, picked up his bass and played the next song. And after that, the entire rest of the show the musicians looked peaceful and the music was beautiful and perfect."

As I walked down Powell Street to the BART after work, my ear was caught by an usually rich mix of voices. An Australian man talked loudly on his cellphone, audible more than a block away, as if his phone was at one end of a hollow tube leading to Sydney and he'd have to shout loudly enough for the sound to reach there. Another man, down toward Market Street, declaimed something loudly in Portuguese, though no one seemed to be listening. And a woman barked orders at her German shepherd in German, though I don't think that enhanced the dog's understanding.

On the BART, a woman was curled up on a pair of seats, her face in a paper bag. Every few minutes, she would look up, jerk her head in different directions like a paranoid owl, then lean back down to the bag. As the Southpaw says in the store when we have clusters of customers like these, "Freak factor: High." But for the BART and the streets of this city, it was just another passenger on just another night.

The Disc That Holds the Memories

12 June 2004

Two young boys, perhaps three and five years old, ran laps around one of the long bins as I spoke to their mother, who seemed unconcerned about their running and yelling. On the third or fourth lap, as I heard them coming up behind me, one on each side, I dropped to a crouch and spread out my arms. As they reached me, I ensnared them, one in each arm, backhand, and said quietly to each, "Please don't run here. There are big people who might not see you, and you could get hurt."

I let them go and they stopped running for a while. Their mother continued shopping, unaffected. A few minutes later, they returned to me, one at a time, and snuggled up on either side of me as I sorted CDs. (I made sure that they weren't trying to get anything from my pockets.) I made eye contact with their mother, who looked down and gave a shrugging smile, but didn't comment. When I had to go help another customer a few aisles over, I put my hands on their shoulders, gave them a warm squeeze, and stepped back and away as they looked up at me and smiled.

When I headed to lunch soon after, I saw that they were again running around, their mother still immersed in her shopping.

Later, another family came to the register to buy some DVDs. Partway through the purchase, the father darted off, carrying the youngest child, to find another DVD. He left the baby carriage and his other son, perhaps four years old, at the register. The boy was right in front of our display of chocolate Lindor balls, in a prime position to cause trouble, so I quietly stepped around in front of the register to observe and, if necessary, to intervene.

Rather than opening or squishing the balls, however, he considered the balls carefully: starting from the lower left tray, and working his way from left to right and from bottom to top, he moved his finger along the tray's printed label, removed one ball from each tray, looked at the color of the wrapping, then held the ball up to his nose and inhaled deeply. He waited a long moment for each, as if holding the scent, then exhaled, placed the ball back in the tray and proceeded to the next one. It struck me that that was just what I might have done at his age.

He finished just as his father returned. To my surprise, he didn't nudge his father to buy him a chocolate. He seemed satisfied just to have seen and smelled them.

A Scottish family showed up early in the morning. As they scattered about the store, the grandmother came to me. She was searching for discs by Savoy Brown, Trace, and Guns N'Roses. The first two were for her son, who wasn't there. "My boy couldn't come with us on holiday, so the least I can do is find the records he's looking for." While we had Savoy Brown, she was pretty sure that he had the discs that we carried. We didn't have anything by Trace. A search of All Music Guide, however, brought up the information that the band was led by Rory Gallagher, and I sold her two of his CDs.

She was buying Guns N'Roses for herself. "I have been to their concerts. I brought my boy to see them some years ago back at Milton Keynes, and I'll tell you I wasn't the oldest one there. Many people with grey hair were there standing in the mud, and we all were dancing to the good rock and roll."

I sold her their new greatest hits package, and tried to interest her in the new album by Velvet Revolver, the band in which most of classic Guns N'Roses lineup plays with the singer from Stone Temple Pilots. She declined. "Yes, that might be quite good and interesting, but this—" she tapped the Greatest Hits CD "—this is the disc that holds the memories."

Sunday Thinks It's Saturday; the Leap Week Staggers, Drunk, Away

14 June 2004

"Spilling things is kind of like tripping."

She Who Laughs said this in one of her few breaths between guffaws, as my supervisor mopped up the remains of a glass of water he'd knocked over in the breakroom. I could almost follow this, though she usually wasn't one to use drug references. But as she continued, a few breaths later, I saw that I had mismapped the simile in hearing her. "It's like when you've tripped, and there's this moment before you actually fall over, and there's the weird look on your face when you know you're about to go down but haven't yet." (Rereading this: did she actually say that part, or did my manager?)

My supervisor sighed, set the plastic cup upright, threw out the soggy paper towels, and sat back down. "My day started with spilling things, and now I'm spilling stuff at lunch. It's just a spilling kind of day."

She Who Laughs laughed even more energetically at this, gasping between melodious swells of compulsive chortling. But I guess there's no harm laughing over spilled water.

Saturday's frantic pace had continued into the evening after I left, with intermittent crises punctuating the time. On the third floor, someone sitting on a window sill leaned back and pushed a pane of glass out, so that it crashed dramatically to the ground. Despite rumors of street people and passersby having been injured in ways that grew increasingly preposterous as the stories grew, no one was nearby or hurt when it landed. And as my manager dealt with covering over the break and cleaning up, one of our more obnoxious regulars, The Maestro (the guy who had flung a Johnny Mathis bin card at me a while back), passed out in the events area and couldn't be roused. He awoke a while later, though, unaware that he had been out.

The Maestro had been a steady fixture at the classical listening stations, though he hadn't been up on our floor in months. I hadn't been aware that he'd been in the store at all, but apparently he'd been coming in again, though staying downstairs. He would always wear his black hair slicked back, dress in a long winter coat and carry a white plastic bag that, on the several times that he forgot to take it with him, turned out to contain clothing and small bottles of the cheapest vodka available. He could often get quite belligerent when interrupted or when a listening station broke down, shouting at people in gusts of explosive anger that spewed out in alcohol-laden breath from between his few remaining teeth. These outbursts had gotten him banned from the store in the past, but with the rapid turnover in security people manning the front door, he somehow manages to continue getting in.

Early in the day, I had stopped into the customer men's room, not wanting to schlep all the way down to the basement to use the employee rest room. As I emerged, Ninja Diva looked up from the third floor information desk. "Was there anyone else in there?"

"One guy," I said.

"An older Asian guy?"

"I couldn't really tell; his sneakers and his pants were around his ankles in the stall. Is he a problem?"

"Well, he's been there for more than half an hour. I've called a manager to check. Was he doing anything weird?"

"Not that I could tell. I heard him blowing his nose, which, I guess, limits what else he might have been doing at the same time."

In the morning, as usual, almost all the customers were either the die-hard regulars who come in every week or tourists. One loud Australian man bellowed to his wife as he wandered around. "We just gotta find that music. That stuff was so real. Gotta get it."

I asked what he was looking for. "We heard this stuff a few days ago, a gospel thing, something like the Abyssinian Anabaptist Church of New Jersey, and it was the real thing, man, not the processed crap, really raw dirty gospel, with people howling and falling over, and you could hear them shouting and hitting the floor and everything. You got that?"

I wasn't sure, but led him to the gospel section and started flipping through it.

"You don't see it, huh? You got any of the real stuff, the grit? All this stuff looks like the music's been cleaned up."

"Frankly, I don't know the gospel section all that well. The person who knows it best isn't here today."

"Well, what good is that? I need to buy the music now. That person should be here."

"It's Sunday morning, sir. I believe she's at church."

"Well, that's just hypocritical of her, isn't it?" He stomped off as I tried to figure out some logic in what he said. But by that point, I wasn't too willing to help him. I was guessing that had Rose actually been there, she might have slugged him by then.

Skimming the Vortex

15 June 2004

Several of us had mysterious stomach ailments throughout the day, despite not having eaten or drunk anything in common. Early in the day, the Southpaw tossed the portable phone to me and made a mad dash to the men's room. Just as he barreled down the escalator, his least favorite customer came up the other way. This woman always has a basketful of items on hold, and comes in to swap items in and out, only rarely actually buying anything. We're never supposed to hold more than a few items for anyone or to hold them for more than three days, but she raises such a ruckus when her holds disappear that we end up holding things for her to avoid the commotion.

She put a couple of new items on hold, removed a few, and promised, as she always does, to return in a few days and purchase some of them. Satisfied, she headed back down just as the Southpaw returned. He grinned with relief when I told him that he had just missed dealing with her. "Then that chili wasn't bad. In fact, it may have been the best damn chili I've ever had."

Material Girl also repeatedly darted down to the restroom toward the end of the day, though she said that she had had ice cream, not chili, for lunch. When we were both at the registers, she complained at length about the rumored new attendance policy, as well as other things that were rumored to be about to change, or, even worse, not to change. We complain to each other a lot; it might just be our common language, both being Jewish.

I told her, though, about an enjoyable customer who had come in over the weekend. He was a drummer, once active but out of service for a while, and starting to try to catch up with what was happening in current progressive rock. I told him about a favorite local band, Metaphor (whose CD we unfortunately don't carry), and *Progression Magazine* (which we had run out of), and convinced him to buy CDs by two very good bands at the edges of progressive rock, Coheed and Cambria and The Mars Volta.

He came back the next day, excited by what he'd heard, and asked me for more recommendations. Since he enjoys King Crimson, I sold him an album by Trey Gunn, who was until recently the bass player for the group. I then referred him to Shredder for more recommendations, since he knows other areas of the field.

Material Girl was pleased by the story. "That's when this job's really good. You get right down to it, it's all about turning people on to music."

She had seen Madonna in concert on Wednesday night, and, as expected, enjoyed the show. Inspired by some of the images and some of what Madonna had said in the past few years, she asked me for a good introduction to Kabbalah. The store was out of my favorite intro, Adin Steinsaltz's *The Thirteen Petaled Rose*. She had spotted Gershon Scholem's *On the Kabbalah and Its Symbolism*, but that would be too much for an intro. My first choice of what we had, David Cooper's *God is a Verb* seemed a bit heavy for a start. I finally settled on *Honey from the Rock*, which struck me, on skimming, as a breezy but adept introduction for those with little background, and as something that would address the areas that would most interest her. She seemed a bit put off by the bits of Hebrew scattered in the text, but I assured her that the English translation of each bit was immediately before or after it.

Late in the evening, some other musicians came in, looking for several bands whose CDs we didn't have, in addition to the new Beastie Boys, which wouldn't be available until the morning. (Almost all CDs and DVDs are released on Tuesdays, and there are severe consequences if anyone sells them early, regardless of how many gazillion copies might be sitting in the back room. Someone once offered one of our workers round-trip tickets to London if he would get him a CD a few hours early, but he refused.)

They mentioned that they would be playing at the Warfield Theatre on Tuesday night. Having seen a picture of P.O.D., I'm pretty sure that they weren't from that band, which means they were probably from Blindside, Hazen Street, or Lacuna Coil. If the latter, Zombie Boy would probably regret not having worked today, since he's been spinning their latest disc quite frequently at work.

Come Together

16 June 2004

Sometimes things just come together.

As I mentioned Monday night, some musicians came through the store and mentioned that they would be playing at the Warfield on Tuesday. When I came home, I dug around the Web and discovered that four bands would be there, including one of Zombie Boy's favorites, Lacuna Coil.

When I got to work on Tuesday, I told him about this. He hadn't heard about it, and decided that if tickets were available, he had to go to it. A few minutes later, I found a note on the information desk that the Southpaw had written down from a call from a label representative. He had just gotten last-minute tickets to a show by some of his label's acts. While the note didn't mention Lacuna Coil, since they are on a different label, I recognized the names of the other acts and realized that it was the same show. I got word to Zombie Boy and to our supervisor, who made the necessary calls. The connection worked. The two of them attended the show.

I had a couple of weirdly erroneous requests Tuesday night that I was able to figure out. One customer was incensed that we not only didn't have any copies of Victoria de Los Angeles's performance of

Chausson's "Songs of the Auvergne," we didn't have any record-ings of it at all. I told him as diplomatically as possible that while we indeed didn't have any recordings of a piece of that name by Chausson, we did have several recordings of Canteloube's settings, including a famous one by that singer.

Another customer insisted that we were missing all recordings of works by Ibeniz, which he pronounced with the sort of slowed-down exaggeratedly perfect Castilian accent that only people who have learned just a few words of a language use to show off. For-tunately, I was able to unpack this as a request for the works of Albeniz, including his "Iberia."

Drama

18 June 2004

Toward the end of the day, I asked a large man in a muscle shirt and wearing a dense mustache if he needed help finding anything.

"Where is Drama?" he asked.

"We have it here on this wall, but it's everywhere in this city."

"Ah," he laughed. "I call that Action/Adventure."

Ruby and Jack

19 June 2004

When Jack came into the store this morning, guided by a friend, he was shaky and close to tears. He came over to where I was helping another customer. "I got a message that there's a DVD waiting for Ruby. I don't know if you heard, but she's had brain surgery twice and is comatose, and they're only giving her a fifty percent chance. I have to get the movie for her."

The other customer nodded and stepped back, and I went to the register with Jack and his friend to retrieve the movie. "It's just been so hard," he said. "I think the only way I've been able to keep together even this much is to sort of convince myself that none of this is really happening."

Jack and Ruby have been regulars at the store since I've worked there, usually coming in on Sunday mornings and heading over to

Rose, with whom they've grown close. They're a striking couple, hard to forget once you notice them. Ruby is an African-American woman, with a warm, round face, a constant, gentle smile, and a signature hat which looks like it has relaxed into a comfortable perfect fit after being worn for a long time. Jack is white, about the same height, with a mostly-grey beard, walking with a cane and a pronounced limp.

They're an ideal couple, moving together as a unit, though often heading to different parts of the music floor to shop for their particular interests. Often, though, one will pick up something for the other and buy it surreptitiously as a present. If Ruby knew that Jack were buying something for her ahead of time, she would protest that he shouldn't, and vice versa. But they have kept up a steady stream of small gifts to each other, presented as already purchased faits accompli.

But a week or so ago, Ruby suffered some sort of attack (I've forgotten exactly what) in her brain, and was rushed to the hospital. And now she's had the two surgeries and is in a coma.

As Jack paid for the DVD, he said, "I'm getting this because she had already ordered it, and I have to believe that she'll wake up and watch it."

"Well, we're all quite fond of her, and pulling for her," I said. "And we're all looking forward to seeing her here again."

Jack came a step closer to crying, then recovered his voice. "It really means a lot to hear you say that," he said. Then he took the bag with the DVD and, with the help of the other man with him, hobbled off to the elevator, and to another long day keeping vigil by his wife's bedside.

This Father's Day

21 June 2004

Sunday was quiet at work. The only customer who stands out, as I try to remember the day on Monday morning, was one wraith-like man who moved slowly around the music floor for a couple of hours. He seemed immensely old, his face a wrinkled cross between Charles de Gaulle and Jimmy Durante. All his clothes were white, including his impeccable suit, shoes, cap, and shirt. When we asked if we could help him, he just shook his head. I suspect that if he had spoken, we would have heard a European accent, but I don't know which kind. As Zombie Boy said, "He's an old gentleman. He looks like he's decided that it's his time to pass on, and has dressed for the occasion."

Quite often, the street people, in attempting to ingratiate themselves so they can convince people to give them change, will try to say something to each corresponding to the person and the season. On Sunday, several of them said "Happy Fathers Day" to me. I was taken aback that they said that, but then remembered that, yes, I do seem like someone to whom someone would be saying that. It's continually hard to believe that I am about the same age as the parents of many of my friends.

I often get the feeling that there must be parallel universes out there in which alternate versions of ourselves have taken different choices. And I keep imagining that there's a universe nearby in which I married (whom?) in my mid-twenties, live in a house in a suburb, and spent Sunday visiting my alternate-universe kids at a college, or at least getting phone calls from them on my day off from some rewarding and reasonably well-paying job in the social services. (In another glimmer of a universe, I am a Rabbi, in another a teacher, and in several others finding a pleasant niche in computing. And, as Anya says, "there's a world without shrimp.")

But here I am, continually single in a world where the years just sort of pile up. At least I remembered to call my father yesterday. I only got to leave a message on his cell phone voice mail which, knowing his uncertain relationship to post-1950s technology, means that he may or may not know that I had called.

Name That Tune

24 Jun 2004

My ability to name tunes isn't as good as it once was. When people come in singing fragments of songs for us to identify, I usually refer them over to Rose or the Southpaw.

But, as part of the ridiculously large (and only mildly glitchy) database of music stuff in my head, I'm still pretty good at remembering tunes, if not lyrics. Over the past few days, I've ended up singing to customers fragments of songs by Sarah McLachlan, Yngwie Malmsteen, When in Rome, and Mocedades, to help them remember what the songs were. Rose, however, continually reminds me that it sounds like I'm singing the Cantorial remixes.

Rose spoke to Jack on Tuesday, and the word on Ruby seems a tiny bit better. It turns out that her coma has been medically induced after the surgery. The trouble started when a brain tumor started to bleed. The two surgeries addressed that, and she's being given the maximum opportunity to recover without further complications. The situation is still extremely risky, but there's room for optimism.

Continental Topic Drift

26 June 2004

It was a quiet day at the store, with people actually getting needed work done. My biggest challenge was a customer that only spoke

Italian, with a few random words of English. I had a hard time communicating to him that some of the CDs that he wanted were out of print, but that we could order others.

When he came to the register, he pointed to one of his CDs and asked, "This CD, it is finished, yes?" I had no idea what he meant, and just looked confused. "This CD, this CD-ROM, is finished? Is terminal?" I remained baffled. But he bought the CD anyway.

I wished She Who Laughs had been there, since she has been studying Italian for several years. The Pippick was surprised when I told her this. I told her that She Who Laughs actually has surprising depth and knowledge, but hides it well under her facade of dippy shallowness. The Pippick marveled at the amount of effort She Who Laughs apparently puts into ensuring that people will underestimate her.

(And when I headed to lunch, the Dancing Guard greeted me, entirely at random, in fluent Italian. He then informed me that one of our supervisors, who was actually on our floor as I was struggling to understand the customer, also speaks the language. He and I are discussing pooling our efforts to compile a list of employees who can translate, at least a little, from different languages, as I've been trying to do since I started there.)

One worker has taken to wearing an elegant blue mesh scarf at work. On the first day that she wore it, it kept tangling with a bracelet on her left wrist. I suggested to her that she should consult with She Who Laughs, who really knows how to accessorize.

When I told She Who Laughs, she was surprised and pleased, and said that she was honored that I would think of her to help with that. As we talked, she went through an incredibly complex ritual of checking her makeup ("because that's what I do"), involving lipstick, mascara, something for her face, and something else about her lashes (I admit to not being makeup-literate). When she was done, I couldn't see much difference, but that probably means that the makeup was successful in not calling attention to itself.

Chapter 14

Rose visited Ruby in the hospital this week, and was daunted by what she saw. Ruby's room is filled with computers and instruments, with a lot of connections between her and the machines. The doctors aren't saying to anyone but family what the prognosis is, but the feeling that Rose reads (and she is one of the best people-readers I know, to an almost scary degree) is, at best, cautious.

Still, Jack is carrying on as well as he can. Some of his friends who had been here to help have had to return home, and he's getting some day to day things done. He told Rose that he had dug out the checkbook and paid some bills. Rose said that she imagined Ruby coming out of the coma, looking at him and immediately asking if things were under control. Jack said that, at this point, he would love just to hear Ruby say anything again.

I'd mentioned to Rose that I'd posted about them to my blog, and that some folks had emailed that they were praying for Ruby. She's passed word on to Jack, who appreciates it.

CHAPTER **15**

_____

_____

The Rainbow Connection

28 June 2004

We had been talking about Mister Rogers, a topic that came up oddly often. Early in the day I had been talking to somebody about jazz piano, and either I or the other person compared someone's music (Vince Guaraldi?) to that on Mister Rogers's show. Midday, I came upon two coworkers as they were talking about him in the context of neighborhoods.

This time, I was telling the Southpaw that I had just seen a customer with a shoulder bag bearing the logo of Mr. McFeeley's Speedy Delivery. He immediately knew that he had to get one, and when the customer came by, he hailed her and asked where she had gotten the bag. It turns out that she had been in Minneapolis when a museum tour of paraphernalia from the show came through, and she had snared the bag there.

Chapter 15

The customer had been relatively easy to spot, since she was walking around with a rainbow flag on a hazardously pointy staff sticking out of her back pants pocket. Even more so than usual, the city was awash in rainbow colors, since Sunday was the annual Gay Pride parade. The parade was huge, I'm told, going down Market Street a few blocks from the store. I saw none of it, however, since I was working all day and didn't even step outside for lunch.

The sidewalks were still crowded as I headed out of work after 5 PM. There were couples everywhere: some gay, some lesbian, some straight, and some where one or both partners were androgynous enough that I couldn't tell. Come to think of it, given the number of people in drag either way (going into the customer bathroom in the afternoon, I saw two apparent women and momentarily panicked, until I assured myself that there were indeed urinals to my right and I hadn't wandered into the women's room by mistake), I might have been wrong about even those couples where I thought I could tell the gender. Quite often, in the evenings when I work, the Guitar God will point out the women who he believes to be men; I tend not to have noticed, partly because I'm prone to missing such clues, and partially because I'm quite willing to accept customers as who or whatever they wish to present themselves as being.

The day was punctuated by several wonderful smiles. Early in the day, a group of women, who apparently didn't know each other, managed to quietly and efficiently shift around, like shapes in a kaleidoscope, so that all of the odd large objects that they were carrying to the parade fit together on the train.

Late in the day, as I stood talking to Ms. Broadway during a break, Kid Howler ran past and, uncharacteristically, smiled and waved at us. Though Ms. Broadway is less fond of Kid Howler than I am, I have a feeling that they've hit a sort of rapport. When the kid makes a mess in the children's section, leaving books strewn about, Ms. Broadway reprimands her and gets her to put the books away neatly. As, she says, someone who grew up with twenty cousins, she doesn't take kindly to people causing trouble like that.

And I have a feeling that Kid Howler might appreciate someone caring enough about what she does to call her on her misbehavior.

In the break room, She Who Laughs zoomed about, her smile even broader than usual. She seemed thrilled about her new second job, as a receptionist at an investment firm. Someone joked that she had gotten the job to hunt for a man, and she laughed and said that there were indeed some great looking guys there. That She Who Laughs was smiling and laughing wasn't news, of course, but it was good to see her honestly happy rather than wearing apparent glee as armor.

On the way back down to the BART, I exchanged an extended smile with a young girl, maybe eight years old, as we waited on opposite sides of a street for the light to change. Her long blond hair was carefully braided, with a single strand of thread in each braid. Looking more closely as we passed crossing the street, I saw that there were seven braids, and that each thread was a different color, in the order of the rainbow.

As I got on the train, I had to step around an old man who was sitting on a folding chair. A tall board rested against the back of the chair, with necklaces, pendants, and other art made from rainbow-colored sets of glass beads hanging from.

Another man, apparently quite drunk, got on the train next to me. He wore jeans that rode quite low on his hips, and a too short t-shirt that exposed his rounded tattooed beer belly below its edge. He stopped short, looked at the wall of beads, and bellowed, "Those beads! You make those, man?" The old man in the chair nodded. "Oh, man," the drunk man said, "you're just beautiful, man! You're like Christina Aguilera, like that song, you know, 'Beautiful,' you're Christina Aguilera, man!"

The train lurched forward, and he started to fall. I caught him with one arm, precariously maintaining my balance by holding onto an overhead rail with the other. He leaned up against me (as I remained vigilant that nothing odd was happening to my wallet), smiled beatifically at me, and said, "You're beautiful, too, man."

I grinned back at him, and shifted my weight until he was standing upright again. By that point, the train was quite crowded, and I had trouble keeping my own balance, not having enough room to put my feet into an effective Subway Surfer Stance (one foot pointed forward, the other at right angles behind it, much as when fencing). But the people on the train were supporting each other and moving around to give others room to balance, either on their own or against others, much like a gentle mosh pit or slow contact improvisation.

M-m-m-my Generation

30 Jun 2004

I find myself getting peeved when much younger coworkers address me as "Sir." It may be that it breaks my illusion of being the same age as everyone else and thus alienates me a bit. On the other hand, I find myself addressing my oldest coworker, who I guess to be in his late 60s, as "Sir." And I suddenly realized while saying that to him on Sunday that the difference between my age and that of many of my coworkers was about the same as the difference between his age and mine.

On the other hand, when the Southpaw said "Excuse me, sir," when we almost collided coming around a blind curve in different directions on Monday, it didn't bug me. He is, after all, from the South, where politeness is a reflex response, and he's not all that much younger than I am.

I'm continually thrown by people's reactions to music from before their time. On Monday, when I asked a customer if I could help her, she deferred to a girl of about ten who was standing beside her. "I'm looking for Mung—... um... do you have music from... when?" She looked up at her mother. "The Seventies?" her mother asked.

"Follow me," I said, and led them to the rock collections. "Are you looking for 'In the Summertime' by Mungo Jerry?"

"How did you know that?," the mother asked.

"Well, if you say the Seventies and 'Mung', there aren't many other ways to complete the name."

"It's her favorite song," the mother said. "She's always singing it, and wanted to get her her own copy."

Digging through the Seventies collections, I found them several anthologies with the song, though they ended up not buying any of them.

While my younger coworkers all have some familiarity with music from the early to mid-Seventies, many have odd gaps. Interestingly, several don't see their own gaps as odd, but wonder how others could have different ones. One who had never heard Genesis before *Invisible Touch* had derided another for being utterly unfamiliar with Roger Waters era Pink Floyd. And as we played some older discs from our Rock Essentials sale, some were amazed by work that they'd never heard from King Crimson and Led Zeppelin.

On the other hand, when I was their age, I had no sense of music from the Fifties. But it seems to me (and this may just be a defensive rationalization) that popular music underwent a break in styles in the late Fifties and early Sixties which plowed over much early popular music, and that there hadn't been such a clear break since then.

When I got a chair and bag from Ikea after seeing them in Zombie Boy's room, and mentioned to the Southpaw that Zombie Boy and I had had some oddly parallel experiences in high school, though a couple of decades apart, he said that I might end up turning into Zombie Boy. "Next thing I know, you'll have gotten tall, pale, and thin and will be wearing his black nail polish."

But now, after some sort of goofy goings-on in a Dungeons and Dragons evening, the Southpaw is wearing Zombie Boy's nail polish. He doesn't, however, seem to have gotten any taller, paler, or thinner (not that he is particularly short, dark, or heavy now).

I had a problem helping one young girl today who was looking for an R&B album. She had a serious stammer and (perhaps because of it) spoke quite softly. Since I often stammer myself, I tried to be quite patient with her, but she had hit a particularly difficult problem: she was looking for "thhhhe c-c-c-d-d-d-d b-by j-j-jo-jo-jo." (Actually, in trying to say "CD," the 'c's came about half as quickly as the 'd's, but that's hard to notate in text.)

There are now popular albums by two different R&B singers, each using just a first name, Joe and Jo-Jo. After she tried several times, I still couldn't figure out which she wanted. I was about to head to the info desk and get a pen and paper for her to write it down when her mother showed up and confirmed that she wanted the one by Jo-Jo, a copy of which was right on the display beside us.

Another customer asked if we could help her find a rap song she had heard. The group was performing it live, and it included the words, "Put your hands in the air and wave them like you just don't care." For those of you haven't groaned instantly: that's like trying to find the blues song that has the line "I woke up this morning," or the song that that opera guy sings that's in, like, Italian.

And a customer on Monday night, who spoke very little English was looking for a children's DVD. She said that the cover had "sun with smile of baby and people in colors." I couldn't guess what she wanted. She then took a pen and some paper, drew a square, and put in it a circle high in the loft corner ("This is sun") and, along a horizon line toward the bottom, several blobby figure '8's ("This is people").

I stared at it for a moment, took the pen, asked, "Is it like this?" and drew a triangle above the head of one, a circle above another, and a vertical line above a third.

"Yes!," she beamed. "This is this!"

"OK," I said. "It's the Teletubbies." But unfortunately we didn't have anything of theirs in stock.

Nil Nisi Bono

5 July 2004

One well-dressed man, after picking out some Eva Cassidy and Chinese music, said: "I'm meeting in three weeks with someone named Bono, who I understand to be a popular musician who is getting into investment banking. Would you recommend any introductions to his current music?" I led him to the U2 bin, where he bought the latest album, holding off until later for the hits compilations.

Our most incoherent customer statement came from a couple who came rushing in to get a particular James Bond DVD: "It can't be out of print—we took a cab down here to get it!"

Another customer got to talking at length about the new Spider-Man movie, which everyone says is excellent. "The marketing on this is wonderful. If you see the image on the actress's face on the poster, it's irresistible. It's absolutely the look of a woman having sex."

"Hmm," I said. "I can't say that I remember."

He picked up the CD and pointed to the picture on the cover. "Isn't that look absolutely torrid?"

"Um, yeah, I guess it is." Actually, I remembered the picture rather well, but the comparison still remained blurry.

It's a Laugh

5 July 2004

She Who Laughs slapped a large cookbook down on the breakroom table. "I really want to get this book," she said. "All you need for any of them is four ingredients."

"Yeah," someone replied. "But you still need to get the four ingredients."

"All you need is earth, air, fire, and water," I said. "From there on, it's just a matter of getting the right spells."

She Who Laughs laughed then frowned. "I don't understand that."

"It's intellectual humor," I said.

She looked askance at me, but then our eyes met gently and she broke into a warm smile. "I love Joe," she said. "Do you know I love him? Joe and I, we've got something special going on."

"Yeah," I said, "she and I have a weird and wonderful thing between us."

Earlier, I heard her talking to another coworker. "So when are we going to do the comedy club thing? I want to laugh!"

"You always laugh," he said.

"But I want to laugh because I want to laugh, not because... "

"Not to hide?"

"I want to laugh at something that's funny, not... not just to laugh." And then she laughed loudly, the pitch a bit higher and fluctuations a bit faster than before.

It's About That Time

6 July 2004

The man stood silently for a long time near the DVDs, eyes closed, head raised toward the stereo speakers on the ceiling, hands clasped at his chest obscuring the fashion logo on his t-shirt. After a while, he looked down, and stepped over to where I stood near the New Releases. "Dude," he said, "this jam is hella chill!"

That may have been the most compactly Californian sentence I had ever heard.

"Yup," I said. "Great stuff."

"What band is this?" he asked.

"It's Miles Davis."

He didn't appear to recognize the name. "I can tell these dudes have been listening to their Phish and, like, maybe, some real old Steely Dan."

"Well, I'd be willing to bet Phish and Steely Dan listened to this."

He frowned and looked at the ceiling again. He looked like he was trying to figure out something that wasn't quite clicking. "They were... how the hell old is this?"

"1969."

"1969? That's before I... That's like forty—uh, thirty—Damn!"

I reached over to the Now Playing rack and handed him the copy of *In a Silent Way* that I had placed there. "OK, jam bands, fusion, electronica—it all pretty much starts here."

"Damn!" he said again. "OK, I gotta get this." He headed to the register and slapped the disk down on the counter, along with disks by Widespread Orchestra, Santana, and Ray Charles, and DVDs that I don't remember.

As I rang him up, he looked at the speakers again, as if trying to absorb the music. "When you've listened to this a few times," I said, "come on back. I've got a lot more music you gotta hear."

"Thanks, Dude!" he said, and wandered to the escalator, where he stood, listened, and smiled, until he headed off downstairs.

It's Purple!

7 July 2004

Yesterday, a man asked me what good CDs were around. When I asked what he liked to listen to, he said, "Well, I'm a Jewish homosexual from the Lower East Side who is the the same age as Madonna —I mean Esther—so take it from there." I told him that that would suggest that his tastes would strongly correlate with mine, and he might like just about anything. I did make some suggestions, though I don't know what he ended up getting.

A little girl in a black and red brocaded dress dragged her mother to the information desk and asked if we had any recordings of *Gypsy*. We went to the Soundtracks area, and I showed her the discs starring Ethel Merman, Rosalind Russell, and Bernadette Peters. She stared at them for a moment, then handed the Peters recording to her mother. "This is the best," she said definitively.

"Why?" her mother asked.

She looked at her mother as if it didn't need explaining. "It's the best. It's purple!"

Later, a woman moved down the Lifestyle music (formerly New Age) aisle, looking at discs while twisting back and forth on her left foot and swirling the hand on her outstretched right arm in circles. When she noticed me noticing her, she looked over at her hand then at me, shrugged, smiled, and said "Yoga."

A man told me, when we were in the Jazz area, "I search DVD of young jazz guitar." When I asked the guitarist's name, he said "Twenty." I couldn't seem to get across the idea of what "name" meant, and since I couldn't tell from his accent what his native language was, I wasn't able to see if I knew the word in that language. Later, it struck me that he might have been looking for a DVD for a jazz guitarist who is twenty.

Tuesday morning, I got trapped in conversation with a classic slow talker. He had heard a singer on *A Prairie Home Companion* whose name he recalled as "Inge Sorenson." (I now see that her name actually is Inga Swearingen.) His description of her, delivered at about one word per second, included a stream something like "a voice that's full yet spare, not stark, like raindrops when it's kind of foggy out, and rich, like an alto flute or a trumpet played low or maybe more like a flugelhorn when played in jazz that's like chamber music but still swings like Cole Porter but without the way that that can be tacky, sounding beautiful, kind of like Cassandra Wilson, but not that low, since I don't like singers who sing as low as she does. . . " Before the sentence trailed off completely, I had missed two calls on the portable phone, each having rung several times then gotten shunted to another phone while I tried to find a polite way to get him to pause.

A few minutes later, a woman began yelling at the man who was shopping with her. "The Beach Boys? You don't even like the Beach Boys! Are you buying things just to be buying them again? You always do this, and you get home and you don't know why you bought them, and you know we live too far from this store and by the time we can get back to return them, you'll have lost the receipt and we'll be out the money and they'll sit on the shelf with all the other crap that you buy and don't use. . . " They were walking together when she started her rant. A few phrases in, however, he stopped and stood near the information desk, arms crossed, looking pained yet amused. She plowed on ahead, not realizing that he wasn't following her. By the time that I lost track of her, she was clear across the floor, heading toward the registers, mercifully out of earshot.

Island of Lost Girls

7 July 2004

Toward the end of the day, I approached a couple who had just come up to our floor. When I asked if I could help them find anything, the woman stepped aside, revealing a black haired young girl of about six. "Ask her," she said. "She's the one with the gift card." At this point, I forget what she asked for, but I headed over to the R&B section with her. The parents didn't follow. "You go on ahead. We'll be here in jazz or something."

I headed back toward the register, almost getting there when a blond girl of about twelve clomped up the escalator in a very short skirt and loud shoes, carrying a much smaller girl on her shoulder. "Can I help you?" I asked.

"Yeah," the larger girl said. "You can carry her for a while."

"I'm sorry," I said, "but I don't think I'm allowed to do that." The girl grunted and unceremoniously dumped the smaller girl on the floor. The smaller girl picked a CD out of the rack and proceeded to hit the larger girl's shoes with it.

As I tried to figure out if I should get her to stop, the first girl reappeared from the R&B section. "Where do you have Wyclef Jean?" she asked (pronouncing the last name as in English rather than as in French). "He isn't under 'Y'." I headed back to R&B with her, and showed her his bin (under 'J').

I almost made it back to the register when yet another tall young girl came up the escalator. She had one arm raised high, holding the hand of the little girl who had been dropped on the floor. The little girl dangled by her hand above the ground like a doll, giggling. The tall girl dropped the little girl onto the floor. (The little girl had apparently gotten good at such landings.) "Isn't anyone watching anything here? This kid was trying to run down the up escalator. She coulda been killed!" She turned and stomped back downstairs.

The little girl stood and looked up at me. I looked around and saw blond hair just visible over the edge of the rock collections bin at the far end of the store. "Come on," I said. "Your sister's down here." We walked toward her. The little girl raised her hand, wanting me to hold it as I walked with her, but I just stayed close and moved along at her pace.

When we rounded the bend to the rock collections, I saw that the blond head actually wasn't her sister, but yet another girl (the fifth one on the music floor then, I think). That girl saw us and took off her head set. "This CD won't play!" she said. "I want to hear this Evanescence CD, please!"

"I'll be right back," I said.

"How can we buy things if we can't listen to them?" she sighed. I walked off, with the little girl beside me, still in search of her sister.

Material Girl, back from her break, spotted us, figured out what was going on, and spotted the sister off at a far corner, near the DVDs, talking with a boy. "She's over here," she called, pointing her out.

I went over to the sister, the little girl still following me, dodging yet another request from the girl in R&B. The sister looked up, startled, when I got there. "Could you please keep an eye on your little sister?" I asked. "She was playing on the escalator, and could get hurt."

"What?" the sister asked, and looked down at the little girl. "Oh, yeah. Her. Sure. C'mon." She picked her sister up by the waist, and slung her under one arm. She stomped off, still talking, unconcerned, with the boy. (After work, I saw the two girls with what I guessed were their parents out on Powell Street. The parents were talking to each other in what sounded like an Eastern European language that I couldn't place, appearing to ignore the girls, though the mother had the little girl's hand clutched firmly in her own.)

I headed back to R&B to help the girl there, but she had wandered back to her parents, who were still in jazz. The girl in rock had headed off to another headset, dancing to a CD that actually seemed to be playing through it. Other than them and the boy who was still by the DVD cabinets, the floor was clear.

It was the end of my shift, so I handed off the phone and keys to Material Girl and headed downstairs. On my way out of the store, the guard looked up and said, "You looked fried. Long day?"

"The store is swarming with little girls, unsupervised. There's thousands of them. One almost got eaten by the escalator."

"Difficult time?"

I sighed and headed off. "You have no idea."

Irving and Cheese

9 July 2004

Some years ago, a headhunter surprised me, when I returned her call from a friend's house as we were about to sit down to dinner, by guessing, correctly and as a total non-sequitur, that we were having macaroni and cheese and apple pie. I took the job.

Last week, another headhunter called me unexpectedly, offering me a technical writing position documenting the installation of computer systems, a two year contract paying four times what I'm earning now. I turned them down cold.

It wasn't so much that the job would have required moving to Irving, Texas (which, despite its bad reputation among people out here— well, the acting President has done so much to turn people against Texas in general that it's surprising that the good people of Crawford haven't run him out of town—is a nice place). I have fond memories of the town, and, come to think of it, I was in Irving when I took that first headhunter's call, at the home of friends who since then seem to have dropped off the map.

The issue was this: For more than a year now, I've been working directly with customers, and making several people happy each day. The thought of sitting in a cube all day, writing materials that no one would read except when things went wrong, and which most readers would resent, made me shudder. Better to stay here, earning little money and doing work that I love.

Still, it would be good to earn more money. I'm sitting here with about three dollars in my pocket (two dollars of it in quarters) and eight dollars in the bank. I get paid tonight, so it's not a significant problem. I had to opt out of getting a shop to look at my car for another week since, if they had been able to fix the broken seat on the spot, as I suspect they might, I wouldn't have been able to pay them for even the labor right away.

It would have been tempting to take the offered job and tell myself that I would save up a lot of what I'd earn and use it to move back here again. But it would involve wasting two years living alone and doing work that I hate. And I know, from having earned close to that kind of money before, that I wouldn't save it. Driving around, hanging out in record stores, and going out to eat for every meal in attempts to evade the oppressive loneliness of returning to a night alone, I would end up squandering the money almost as quickly as I would earn it.

CHAPTER **16**

The Passengers

9 July 2004

I spent most of Wednesday wandering about the city with Zombie Boy. Like me, he isn't much of a fan of solitude, so seeing a day when neither of us were busy and I was going to be in the city anyway, I suggested that we get together.

Zombie Boy and I agreed to meet at the Civic Center BART station at about 1:30. I got there a few minutes early and called his cell phone from mine. He gave me simple directions to his place. (I'd been there on the night that I didn't get home, but I'm terrible at remembering where things are in the best of circumstances.) He decided to head out before I got there, and with a couple of more phone communications, we managed to zero in on each other. When I saw him across Jones Street, I bellowed his name loudly enough to startle the crowd of people slouching and drinking by the wall of the building that I was passing. He spotted me, waved, and darted through the light traffic, mid-block, to where I was.

We wandered vaguely downtown, intending to eat, possibly in North Beach, and to see some interesting buildings. He's a fan of earthquake-era San Francisco history, and rattled off all sorts of interesting information and anecdotes about the places and street names we passed. He pointed out several buildings with surprisingly detailed exterior designs, and how the more recent buildings seemed bland by comparison.

We wandered through the Ferry Terminal market for a while, tasting samples of odd foods we could never afford, then, much hungrier, hopped the MUNI F Train to Fisherman's Wharf. Skipping most of the tourist joints (we dropped into the Hard Rock Café store where Rose has a second job, though we knew she wasn't there), we headed for In-N-Out Burger, but got waylaid and ended up at Joe's Crab Shack, where we spent far more money than we could justify on more fried food than either of us had eaten in the past year or so. (I was so stuffed that I forgot to eat dinner, and had to remind myself to eat breakfast in the morning.)

Zombie Boy pointed out several fascinating things happening just outside the window, none of which I noticed until he pointed them out. (The most striking was a small bird, caught in a wind current and appearing to fly backwards.) The same was true walking through the city: as much as I try to notice everything that's going on, more gets by me than I can catch, and Zombie Boy, with his very different perceptions, catches an almost entirely different set than I do.

Wandering on toward some more interesting buildings, we spotted another large record store, and I had a hunch that we just had to go in. The store was in mild disarray, with a single employee puttering about. We immediately headed to the Clearance area, where we found a few interesting things, mostly at about $6.99.

When I got several racks over from where we started, though, I spotted a small handwritten sign saying that all discs with orange tags were 99 cents each or three for two dollars. I went over and asked the employee (who seemed momentarily startled to see that he really had customers) if that was only for that rack.

"No," he said, "it's all the orange tags in the store. Box sets, too—they count as one item, so the box sets are three for two, too. And, yeah, let's do it for the green tags, too. My boss is leaving in two days, and we're gonna have to get inventory down, so yeah, have fun." He handed me a shopping basket, and we returned to the racks.

(By the way, I've found that shopping bags and baskets are a wonderful way to connect with customers. We have black mesh shopping bags available for use inside the store, and I frequently dart over to the rack of them, grab one, and head over to customers whose hands are getting full of product. They tend to really appreciate the gesture, even if they decline the offer, and, I think, shop more than they would have otherwise.)

We returned to the racks and began shopping in earnest. Discs that we might not have noticed at $6.99 became must-buy items when priced at less than a tenth of that. We spent more than an hour going through the racks in detail, grabbing unexpected things and frequently running discs back and forth to each other, insisting the other must immediately get something we had spotted. I also picked up a few discs as presents for others. There was a disc of Harold Melvin and the Blue Notes, for example, that I had been insisting that Material Girl needed to know; seeing it on this sale, I grabbed it instantly for her.

Once we had gotten through the racks, we each sat down on the floor and sorted through the discs. I made a stack of definite buys, possible buys, and ones to put back, whittling down until I hit a self-imposed limit of 30 discs, which would cost me 20 dollars before tax. Seeing that we had dropped out of sight, the employee wandered over after a while, saw what we were doing, and said that that was exactly the way that he shops, too.

(And once, within that store, I saw a dowdy woman looking confused in the classical racks, with the employee not noticing. Being too compulsive to let a CD store flounder anywhere, I wandered over, engaged her in conversation, and helped her find what she was looking for. Later, when I saw another customer looking through the Clearance discs, I let her know about the sale. She got excited, and quickly had accumulated a large pile of CDs.)

Crash

11 July 2004

Toward the end of the day, I saw an amusing collision. A couple, walking hand in hand, and noticing little else, snared a completely self-absorbed woman on a cell phone trying to walk between them. The woman, hitting the couple's joined hands with her waist, toppled forward, her cell phone landing on the floor and skittering away from her. The couple's hands remained together, functioning as a sort of fireman's carry, keeping her from falling over and bouncing her back toward standing.

All three looked startled, and muttered apologies. The woman darted around the outside of the couple, retrieved her phone, and continued walking. The couple waited until she was out of view, then broke out into helpless laughter.

Mystery Train

15 July 2004

Heard, verbatim, on speakers on the BART train:

Now arriving at Richmond. What am I saying? This
is the Richmond train. These signs are always flashing
"Richmond, Richmond" at me. But this is MacArthur.
This is MacArthur station. This is the Richmond train,
arriving at MacArthur station.

One of our supervisors emerged from the elevator with a customer.
She had crooked one arm. The customer, carrying a white cane
in one hand and holding the supervisor's forearm with the other,
shuffled gingerly alongside her. They moved together to the register, where the supervisor placed a stack of four audiobooks on the
counter. "Ring these up, please," she said.

"I'll be right here." I started to ring up the sale.

"Do you take Discover?" the customer asked.

I nodded, then audibly said "Yes."

The customer pulled out a small case of credit cards and IDs and
picked through them. Each time that he felt embossed characters
on a card, he raised the card to just above his dark glasses, apparently scrutinizing it with what little vision he had left.

I had no idea how to ring up a completely sightless customer.
(Do they sign credit card slips, or is there an appropriate other
thing for them to do?) When the slip to sign for the credit card
printed out, I placed it and the pen on the counter, sliding them so
that they touched his hand as it rested there. "Would you sign this,
please?" I asked.

He picked up the pen and placed its point on the slip, exactly at
the right place. "Where should I sign it?" he asked.

"Right where it is now," I said.

He picked up the pen again, putting its point down about a half
inch above where it had been. "Um, farther down... " I said.
"Hold on."

I put my hand down so that the tip of the index finger was where
he should sign. The side of the finger rested against the point of
the pen.

161

Without either of us saying anything, he understood my gesture. Lifting the pen from the paper, he carefully slid it along the side of the finger until it reached the fingertip. I raised my finger and he signed there. His handwriting was neat and legible, but the signature still ran at an angle, crossing into the printed information toward the end of the name.

I put the slip in the register, printed out the receipt, and put it and the CDs in a bag. When I held out the bag above the counter, the supervisor reached over and took it. Stepping over to the other side of the customer, she once again crooked her arm, placed the customer's hand on it, and led him back to the elevator.

On the Blue Nile

20 July 2004

Though the days blur, I know that Saturday was quite busy, but about normal for a Saturday. Sunday and Monday were quiet. This may have been caused, in part, by the escalator up to our floor being broken for the past two days. Several times, when I was one floor below, I saw people approach the escalators, look up the stairs of the open one (which, since it had to handle people traveling both up and down, was turned off), and decide not to go up to the floor. On the other hand, I have the impression that the people who made it up there were, on the average, each spending more money and buying more items than most customers do. Maybe they wanted to make the investment in energy that they had made in walking up the stairs worthwhile.

The elevator was working, though as slow as always. One perennially cranky customer, an older woman with a metal cane and an acidic New York accent (the accent of the New York acidim?), stomped down the stairs when she left. "I could die of old age," she said, "before I would catch that elevator."

Which reminds me of what an old man said a few days earlier, while contemplating the expensive box set of *The Complete Ella Fitzgerald Songbooks*: "My wife is telling me 'Buy it now. In two years you may be deaf or dead.' "

One customer came in looking for CDs by The Blue Nile. We didn't have any in, and several appeared to be out of print. As I rattled off the names of the albums for the customer, who was unsure of which to get, another customer, sharply dressed and with a precise British accent, interrupted us at the mention of a particular one. "That's the one you want," he said. "It's their greatest."

I looked more closely at the entry for the CD. "It looks like it's out of print, though, so we wouldn't be able to order it."

"If I may do so, sir, without violating etiquette, might I mention where I saw a copy yesterday?"

"Certainly," I replied.

"All right," he said, turning to the customer. "Go to Amoeba Music on Haight and Stanyan Streets. After you pass the registers, there is a bay of clearance CDs to your left. In the last aisle, just before you would go down the stairs to the main floor, go to the third row from the end. The Blue Nile CD is about a dozen discs back."

"Really?" she said. "You remembered that?"

The customer nodded.

"I can believe it," I said. "I sometimes remember things like that, too. I have to look up my own phone number, but this stuff sticks with some people." It really does: recently, I told someone who was looking for music by the group Shanti Shanti where I had seen a book on the group at another bookstore several months ago, down to how far from the end of a particular shelf of a certain bookcase it was.

"Thank you, sir," the helpful man said. "And my apologies, again, for recommending a competitor."

"Not a problem," I said. "If we can't get someone the music she wants, at least we can try to get her closer to it."

"May I recommend some similar music?" the man said.

"Sure!" the woman replied. They continued their eager conversation as they left the floor together. I love when customers meet like that.

As always, I kept a 3x5 notebook in my shirt pocket, and scribbled notes about other customers and events to reconstruct later here. (Instant memory: just add water. Contents may expand or change shape during storage.)

A girl of about 12 walked to the rhythm of the overhead music in sandals with tall cork soles. For each measure, she stepped forward on the downbeat, then lifted the heel of the back foot on the third beat of four so that the foot was perpendicular to the ground. She tried to look nonchalant doing this, but had problems in balancing with the back toe pointed. Quite often, the opposite arm would shoot out to one side on the upbeat to keep her from toppling.

A woman asked if we had the DVD of Dr. Seuss's *The Lorax*. She was thrilled when I handed her the set of four Dr. Seuss DVDs that included that one. She handed it down to her son, who was about five years old and eyed it critically. "It must have 'the Grinch Grinches.' I am most concerned that it must have 'the Grinch Grinches.' " He was overjoyed when I told him that it did, indeed, have *The Grinch Grinches the Cat in the Hat* (which I had never heard of before). He clutched the set tightly, and literally jumped up and down in glee.

Later, a group of five teenage girls came up to the floor and bought various pop CDs. Each one of them was blond, tanned, bearing a 20 dollar gift card, and wearing jeans, a cropped shirt, and what appeared to be a hospital bracelet with a name and other information typed on it. There had to be some back story behind that (other than an odd choice of accessories), but I decided that it might be rude to ask. Maybe they were a really odd Girl Scout troop, or experimental clones being introduced to society.

My final customer on Saturday was named Leonard Bernstein. Really. I asked if he gets a lot of comments on his name. He said, "A few. Mostly in record stores."

Name

20 July 2004

As I looked up something for a customer at the information desk, I heard him say to his wife, "Now that's an unfortunate name!"

"What name?" I asked.

I looked up, and saw that he was pointing to the display of my *Surprise Me with Beauty*. "Joseph Zitt," he said. "Could that be a real name?"

I smiled serenely at him. "It's been a struggle, but I've learned to live with it."

The lines of the man's face shifted almost chaotically, as he ran through several different emotions and facades. "Oh, boy," he said. "Well, uh, congratulations at being in print!" He paused. "Well, now that I've insulted your name, are you sure that you really want to work in the pop section?"

A few moments later, at the change of the hour, I went over to the register. The couple came over to buy something almost immediately, looked up, and were taken aback to see me there, too. "Weren't you just at the information desk?"

"You remember that *Star Trek* episode where the librarian was everywhere at once? That's me."

"Well, now that we've gone and crossed the picket line at Macy's and insulted an employee here, what would you suggest to complete our day?"

I thought a moment. "Well, you could find a good vegetarian restaurant and complain that they don't have cheeseburgers."

The man laughed loudly. The woman blushed.

Everybody, Get In Line

30 July 2004

The store's current sale is so simple that it confuses people. If you buy one book, you get 25% off one CD. If you buy two books, you get 25% off two CDs, and so on. A boxed set of books counts as one book. A boxed set of CDs counts as one CD. And the 25% is off the list price. If the CD is already on sale, you pay either the sale price or 25% off the list price, whichever saves you more, but you don't get both discounts at once. (And rewriting this paragraph two days later, I've seen that the official mailing blurb from the store says that it's only good for one CD per customer. But when I rang up sales on Tuesday, it worked for one CD per book. Your mileage may vary.)

Still, when I tell people about this, they tend to get a "deer in the headlights" look, roll their eyes back in their heads as they try to remember third grade arithmetic, or squint at me, trying to figure out how we're trying to rip them off.

A young girl came in with what I suspect was her grandmother, looking for the soundtrack to *Bend It Like Beckham*. When I showed it to them, they began a rapid argument in an Eastern European language. The grandmother then shoved the CD at me and said in a dense accent, "This CD, it is cheaper at Costco?" The way she said the name, it rhymed with "vodka," but I was able to make a good guess from the relatively unmangled consonants.

"I don't know for sure," I said. "They have good deals on some things, but they carry fewer CDs than we do, and I don't know how their standard prices are."

The grandmother looked, confused and wary, at the girl, who repeated what I said, translated into their language. She then shook her head and put the CD down. "Too much. We go Costco."

The girl looked up at me, pleadingly. I saw that she was holding some paperbacks, and said, "You know, we have a sale on now. If you buy a book, a CD is 25% off."

The girl again translated for the grandmother. "So how much is now?" the woman asked.

I looked at the price sticker. "Well, the CD is $17.99. A quarter of that is... um... $4.50, so the price is $13.49 if you buy a book."

"But this is with tax? How much tax?"

"Tax is about one twelfth of the price, so that would add up to about $14.75." Actually, it would have been a bit less, but I figured that rounding off to the nearest quarter was the best that I was going to do in my head.

"But we must buy book?"

"Yes. Any book."

The grandmother narrowed her eyes and glared at me. "So what is smallest, cheapest book in store?"

The girl, exasperated, said something to her in their language, pointing to the books she already held. "No," the grandmother said. "They not trick us. You get those books, OK, but we find small cheap book too so we get good bargain."

The girl opened her mouth to say something, but gave up. She looked back at me with a "What can one do?" look as the grandmother dragged her off to look for what she would consider a bargain.

The store was understaffed again today, and when one worker called in sick, the schedule shifted madly about. Since the music department always seems to have lowest priority in staffing, several workers were sent downstairs at various times to fill in gaps in areas that management apparently considered more important. (Well, maybe they have so much confidence in the music sellers that they figure that we can do the impossible easily.)

At noon, a few moments after the encounter with the grandmother, my supervisor called to say that he would be stuck downstairs printing out some needed reports, and that I would be on the floor alone for a few minutes. He had already put up the signs saying that the registers on our floor were closed and directing people to purchase things on the ground floor.

Almost immediately, the portable phone rang. A customer had information on a CD by the New Christy Minstrels and wanted to know if we had it. We didn't but could order another one with even more tracks for the same price. The customer was dubious, since hers was a 3 CD set with 30 tracks, and the one we list was only 2 CDs but had 45 tracks. She wanted to be sure that the one we could get had all of the tracks that hers did. She proceeded to read the track list, one by one, as I checked them against the listing on our computer. Ours did have all 30 tracks, and she ordered it.

As I went through the ordeal, standing at the PC behind the registers, I saw a tiny old woman approach the register carrying a plastic bag. It took her a long time to get there, each of her steps carrying her forward by only two or three inches. By the end of the list of CDs, she had finally reached the register, reached up to the counter (yes, she was really that small), put the bag on it, pulled out a CD Walkman and opened it. She started talking, apparently not seeing that I was on the phone.

The customer on the phone had already started to ask me about more music, but I managed to get her to pause her monologue and put her on hold. I turned to the woman at the counter. "Ma'am, I'll be with you in a moment, once I finish helping the customer on the telephone."

She nodded as if she understood, and said, "The people downstairs said that you would help me. This DC does not play, and I am told that the problems are the batteries, even though I have only had the DC player for six months, and that you will put new batteries in for me." She, too, had a thick Eastern European accent (though she had a better grasp of English grammar), and really did say "DC" for "CD."

"Ma'am," I said again, "I am helping another person who has called me on this telephone," (I held the portable phone down where she could see it), "but I can help you when I have finished speaking with her."

"Oh, yes, another customer. All right, thank you, I'll wait," she said.

I turned back to the computer, and took the customer off of hold. "OK, I'm back. How can I help you?"

"Well, when I was in the store a few weeks ago, I saw that you didn't have anything by the Seekers, and wondered what you could get."

I searched for CDs by the Seekers on the computer. We indeed didn't have anything in stock, but there were several that we could order. Painstakingly, she had me read the information for each one, as well as the complete track listings. As I did so, several other people lined up at the register, all ignoring the signs that said that they were closed.

When I got to the end of the list, I asked if she would like to order any of them. "You must understand," she said, "that this is a very important band, and would be quite popular. If you ask anybody who was in San Francisco in the 60s, and this would include many of us who are in our 60s, including many retiring baby boomers with a significant amount of retirement income that we would like to spend in your store, you would know that they are an important band, and that you should stock all of their records and put them prominently on display."

"I'll keep that in mind," I said. "Would you like to order any?"

"Oh, no," she said. "I already own every note that they ever recorded. But I thought that it would be important for you to know about them. It has been a pleasure speaking with you. Goodbye."

I don't know for how long I stared in disbelief at the phone after she hung up. After that timeless moment, I turned back to the woman with the CD Walkman, looking at the dismantled parts she had strewn across the counter. "You look stressed," said one of the several customers behind her.

I swept a hand across my face, wiping it from a grimace to a smile. "OK, now," I said cheerfully.

My supervisor, finally escaped from the printer room, had come up during the long phone call. "You know," he said, "I would hear about the weird people that would show up and fluster you when you were up here alone, and I thought it might just have been you. But this stuff is as weird as you describe it."

Pedestrian Caught in Freak Balloon Accident

4 August 2004

9:39 PM: Two young girls in matching grey jackets and blue skirts walked northward, uphill, on Powell Street. White ribbons, trailing almost horizontally for several feet behind them, led to pink balloons that bobbled along, at a level with the heads of some passersby. (From a distance, the balloons and heads were almost indistinguishable.)

When they were a couple of yards from me, I heard a sudden shout. Looking for its source, I spotted an old lady, not much taller than the girls, falling to the ground. One of the balloons, shifting about in the breezes, had cut in front of her from one side to the other, snaring her neck and pulling her down.

A man passing next to her when she was snagged caught her with one arm, and unwrapped the balloon and ribbon from around her neck with the other.

The woman appeared unhurt. The girls, who kept on going and never looked back, appeared neither to know or to care what had momentarily blocked the movement of their balloons.

The Safety Dance

10 October 2004

As I came back from lunch, I saw an impressively proportioned woman dancing frenetically at a listening station at the top of the escalator. She stayed there for what seemed like more than the length of a CD, then moved on and resumed her dancing at a station in the rock section.

A man came to the information desk and delivered a high speed rap from which I eventually figured out that he wanted to get promo flats for jazz LPs. He mentioned being from DC, and we rattled off names of Metro stops at each other in some sort of cross-country bonding ritual. We didn't have any of the promo flats, but I directed him to another store down the street.

A while later, a coworker came over and said that a man at the back of the store was describing another customer to someone over a cell phone. Looking and listening (which wasn't hard, since the guy was speaking quite loudly), we realized that he was excitedly describing the woman who was dancing at the listening station at the other end of rock. (As I said to that coworker, when I see a woman dressed like that and moving like that in this city, my first question is whether it really is a woman—but if she wasn't, it was a remarkable work of bio-engineering.)

I thought that talking about someone very loudly in public in the terms that he was using was rather rude, but didn't do anything. When he pulled out a digital camera and pointed it at her, though, I intervened. "Sir, we don't allow people to take pictures in the store."

"Not even of people?"

(I avoided the impulse to say "Especially of people.") "No, sir. There's no angle to shoot anyone without getting at least some copyrighted CD graphics in the picture."

He seemed cowed and put the camera away. But I wouldn't be surprised if he snuck some photos anyway. And I wouldn't be surprised if the dancer wouldn't have minded: I think she was trying, as we were taught in performance classes, to "invite being seen."

Buying the Bear

12 December 2004

We're offering a handsome teddy bear for $7.99 to people who makes purchases larger than thirty dollars. Since he looks rather bookish, with tiny plastic eyeglass frames on his nose, the store calls him Booker Bear. Up on the music floor, however, we call him Booker *T.* Bear.

Today, two big guys in leather jackets came to the counter with a stack of horror movies and metal CDs. I gave them my usual pitch about getting Booker: "Do you know anyone who would love a bear?"

"A bear?!" one of them snorted. "Who the hell do I know who would want—"

He stopped short, picked up the bear, stared at it, then set it down gently on top of the DVDs. "My mom. . ." he said. "She's 94. . . Alzheimer's . . . doesn't remember her own name. I'm giving her a sweater—a cheap sweater, since I know someone at the home's gonna steal it—but this. . . bear. . . it's the one thing I can give her that she'll understand."

I rang him up and packed his stuff in one of the tall grey bags, with the DVDs on the bottom, the CDs stacked above them, and Booker seated on top, his eyes peering out over the top of the bag. I patted the bear on the head. "Bye, Booker," I said. "Be a good friend."

The guy picked up the bag and held it close to his chest. His partner put his arm around him. The guy with the bag rested his head on his partner's shoulder as they walked slowly to the elevator.

CHAPTER 18

"So this deaf guy walks into a record store..."

29 March 2005

There's a bad cold going around the store. As a result of mine (we think), I have temporarily lost much of my hearing. The doctor that I saw today says that it appears that fluid may have built up in both my ears, effectively plugging them.

While I can hear some ranges of sound, I don't get human voices at all, unless they are quite high in pitch or spoken directly to me by someone whose face I can see. (I wonder if I'm doing some unconscious lipreading.) I can hear some others, but not tell what they're saying.

It also blocks much music, since the bulk of the information in most music is in the same frequency range as the voice. At work on Saturday, I was unable to tell, much of the time, whether we had music on the overhead system at all. By Sunday, I was able to tell if it was playing if it was rather loud, though I confused at one point 50 Cent (aggressive rap) for The Postal Service (wispy techno-pop), and could only hear the highest ranges of the voice in Renee Fleming's Handel album.

The sound cut out fairly abruptly Friday night, first in my left ear and then, a little while later, in my right. It was replaced by a vague rushing sound, most in the octave about Middle C, with various sine tones in that octave and above seeming to fade in and out, distributed across the stereo field in an ever-changing chord. It really is quite beautiful, though I look forward to being able to choose not to hear it. (I may try to synthesize a version of it on my computer once this has all passed.) I can also hear the sounds of my body more clearly, especially the internal knocking and clicking of my knees and ankles as I walk. (Have they always been this loud?)

Interestingly, I can understand sounds on headphones quite well, especially if I hold the headphones tightly to my head so that they make strong contact with the skin of the ear or fully block the ear canal. Once I realized this, I tried to hack together an impromptu hearing aid using the Record function of my MP3 player. Unfortunately, it doesn't pass through what it hears to the headphones, so it didn't help. (When I told my housemate this, he said that he could rig some software to do it, but that it would require schlepping around a fragile Mac PowerBook to work.)

The problem is also remixing other sounds around me in peculiar ways. At one point yesterday, I heard an odd chittering sound, bouncing around the space in front of me. I worried that I might be hearing mice, or something like them. But when I turned around, I discovered that I had left the water in my sink running—the usual complex mass of sounds of running water had gotten filtered by the ever-changing sound in my head, so that different frequencies, freed by the shifting tones, appeared to be darting around the room.

Even more oddly, except for the hearing problem and the phleg-mish cough that won't go away, I feel just fine. From how I sound when I talk and my difficulties in communicating with others, it seems like I should be on the verge of falling over. But other than those issues, the cold is gone. I took a long walk this afternoon, and don't feel sick or tired at all (except for being sick and tired of sounding sick and tired).

The difficulty in understanding voices seemed to grow over the course of Saturday—or maybe it was then that I realized that that was where the problem lay. (And it's surprising how hard a time I'm having sorting out the quite brief chronology of this mess. But ordered lists have never been my strength.)

Rose could tell that I wasn't kidding about having trouble hear-ing music early in the day. Being the first person to work the reg-isters, she chose the first music to play overhead. I took me a long time to notice the music playing at all, but when standing directly under the loudest of the speakers in the ceiling, I heard some un-mistakable trumpet notes. I went to look at what she had put in the "Now Playing" rack, and said, "Good, I am hearing Miles." But when she went to put on the next music and replace the CD in the rack, she saw that, while she had played *Kind of Blue*, she had displayed *In a Silent Way*, and I couldn't tell the difference. (For those from the classical side of the aisle: that would be vaguely like mistaking Ravel for Vivaldi. But only vaguely.)

I was still able to use the phone pretty effectively as of Saturday afternoon. When I returned a call from friend in the mid-afternoon, I told her of what I was facing, and she suggested that I try a good Urgent Care clinic that she knew, at the University of California San Francisco complex on Parnassus Hill, along the fabled N-Judah MUNI line. Unfortunately, when she checked with them, they told her that they were closing on Saturday afternoon before I could get there, and that they would be closed on Sunday.

On Saturday night, I flashed on something like this that had hap-pened some twenty years ago. I had a clear image of walking down

7th Avenue in Manhattan with one ear not working. I remembered
that I stopped into a drugstore and got some drops and a blue bulb-
like water syringe for flushing wax out of the ear. (As I picture it
now, I realize that, oddly, I recall having used them in the bathroom
of Coliseum Books, on fifty-something street, but the bathroom itself in my mind's eye is that of the Strand on 8th Street.) In that
case, it worked quite well, getting a glob of wax out and clearing
the hearing up. I resolved to do so again, though with doubts as to
why it would have suddenly happened in both ears at once.

I woke up fairly early on Sunday morning, and went to Long's
Drugs to get the Earwax Removal Kit. I did get waylaid heading
there, though, since as I passed Saul's Deli, I realized that I was
walking past a Jewish (though not kosher) deli on a Sunday morning when it wasn't crowded, so stopping for brunch was surely
some kind of a mitzvah. The lox and eggs that I got was (were?)
wonderful, though the coffee was lousy. And a woman to my left,
who seemed a little addled to start with, kept trying to engage me
in conversation, though I could understand only about one out of
every ten words that she said.

I retrieved the supplies from Long's and headed home. I dili-
gently followed the procedure with the drops and syringe, but it
didn't seem to help much.

Once at work, I found myself to be almost absolutely useless at
the information desk. I had an extremely hard time trying to figure
out what customers wanted, and I think I annoyed several with
my seeming obtuseness. I found working the registers to be much
easier, though, since the interactions are, for the mostly part, quite
ritualized. I arranged to work the registers (a task that I usually
avoid) for as much of the rest of the day as I could. Even then,
I still got questions from the customers. I was able to answer a
surprisingly large number of them from quite little information. (I
have a feeling that our conversations are highly redundant, in a
very good and useful sense.) And coworkers at the other register
helped to answer those with which I had trouble.

Things were complicated somewhat, and decomplicated in others, by the large performance that we had in our Event Space on Sunday. A well-known band, who have had several minor hits and have done acclaimed TV show themes and children's music, played at 4 PM on our third floor. We had the largest crowd there that I had ever seen in the store. Before and after the performance, they mobbed the registers. Fortunately, most were buying either the CD or DVD of the band's latest project. (As the store had hoped, many were also buying unrelated items.) The band had thought one aspect out well: knowing that many of the people who would want to stand in line to get their autographs would have small children who would find standing in line far less fun, they graciously autographed many CD booklets and DVD wrap-cards in advance, and we provided them to people who were buying the CD or DVD if they wished.

I left work Sunday annoyed and frustrated. The grumpiness grew when I went to my favorite Chinese restaurant for dinner. Signs in the windows regretted to inform us that it would be closing on Friday after fifteen years in business. It's the same old story of so many gutted cities: a landlord would rather leave a space empty at an exorbitant rent then have it active and producing a lesser income. Perhaps there's some tax angle involved, but it's building us a ghost town, with more and more dusty rooms where business had, until recently, thrived.

Once I got home, I poked around at some things online, then went to sleep, setting my alarm for quite early to give me time to decide what to do. When I awoke, I did another treatment with the earwax stuff, confirmed that it didn't seem to be helping at all, and planned my day. I called in sick to work (which I really didn't want to do—on top of everything else, today was the beginning of the Classical Music Month promotion, which is my area); fortunately or not, I started coughing just as the manager answered, and he told me to stay home and get better.

I rarely stay home from work. When I do, it's usually because I've gotten myself so sick that I get the clear signal from my body to remain as inert as possible. Today, since I wasn't feeling sick, I had to devote the day to getting better, and that meant going for medical help. In this case, going to a good Urgent Care Center made sense.

Urgent Care Centers, as they're called out here, are somewhat like what we had in Texas, where they were called Minor Emergency Clinics, or, colloquially, "Doc in a Box." They're for things that require immediate examination and handling, but don't require an emergency. The one that my friend recommended, at UCSF-Parnassus, has the added good point that it's a training facility for the medical students. It's relatively inexpensive (and, all things considered, our company's medical coverage is quite good, especially when compared to our lousy pay) and struck me as exactly what I hoped it would be.

Getting there was simple: I took the BART to the Embarcadero station and transferred to the outbound N-Judah MUNI line, which stopped right at the medical center. (I'm pretty sure that the MUNI sound system even announces that stop, though of course I didn't hear the announcement today.) Following the directions that I was given when I called the center, I went into the center complex, followed the signs, took the elevator to the 10th floor—which, the complex being built into a massive hill, is the street-level floor on the Parnassus street side —and followed the signs around to the clinic.

A person at the desk spoke to me briefly, had me fill out a card with information, then told me that he'd call my name when they were ready to see me. I sat down in a comfortable chair in the waiting room, in the sunlight of the large windows, looking across the valley to the trees and buildings on some other distant hill.

After a while, I realized that if I wouldn't hear if they were to call my name, so I checked again with the person at the desk to see if they had called me yet, explaining that I wasn't able to hear announcements. He said that they were on the person just before me, and that he would make sure that I would know that I was being called.

He handed me a clipboard of forms to fill out—identification, authorization, contacts (I listed my roommate as my contact person, since he'd have the best shot at finding the right people and informing them appropriately about whatever might arise), privacy, etc.— and I sat back down within line-of-sight of his desk. (That I was wearing my usual red baseball cap probably also helped my visibility.)

When he was ready, he apparently called my name, but also waved to me from the desk. I handed him the clipboard, which he looked over, then said that another person would call me (and, again, would make sure that I knew that I was being called) in a few minutes. Not long after, someone else appeared at a doorway and called my name—without gesturing, but fortunately her voice was pitched so high that I could guess that she had called my name from the sounds that popped up above the internal blur of noise.

She guided me to an examination room and asked the usual questions about medical history, drugs (prescribed and otherwise), and symptoms. She then left and said that a medical student would be in to see me. The student came in quite quickly, a charming man with perhaps the best bedside manner (which translated in my head to "customer service approach") that I have ever experienced. He was amiable, sympathetic, listened well, communicated well (taking care to be sure that I was hearing him clearly), and knew what he was doing. It also helps, I think, that he had a good musical vocabulary: he understood just what I meant when I said that the noise in my head seemed to be mostly in the octave above Middle C, and that I was able to distinguish The Postal Service from Handel, but not from 50 Cent.

He took a good look at my throat and ears. While there was some clustered wax deep in the left ear, there didn't seem to be any on the right. Still, he (and the doctor that he brought in briefly to take a look) decided to do what they could to loosen the wax on the left, flushing it with a saline solution, and scraping very gently at it with a plastic loop. There wasn't much success, but he said to continue with the over-the-counter earwax removal kit that I was using for that ear.

(Looking at the box, I see that the ear drops are Carbamide Peroxide. In telling him about it, I got the name wrong, and told him that it was Corbomite Peroxide. He apparently knew what I meant, and neither of us noticed what I now see was an unintended *Star Trek* reference.)

He gave me a prescription for something that would address the fluid within the ears (30 blurs of squiggle, with a note to division-sign mumble squiggle each time) and a form saying that I saw a doctor and should stay out of work for the next three days. (This was necessary so that the whole set of days off work would count as a single occurrence; otherwise, each would use another one, which are in rare supply.)

As I emerged from the BART, I realized that I had forgotten to turn my phone back on after shutting it off at the medical center. There were two messages. I recognized one as being from my father, who is currently in a rehab center recovering from a recent incident of some sort that put him in the hospital again. The other was from my stepmother. As usual, my father's tone was plaintive, and my stepmother's was somewhere between browbeating and complaining. I couldn't understand a word that either said, and won't be able to return the messages until my hearing clears. (And I don't have another medium to reach them, since my father can't get at his email and my stepmother has steadfastly avoided being set up with modern communications.) [Update: my father called later, at midnight my time, 3 AM his time, and we were able to talk for a bit; his voice has also grown quite high-pitched in recent years, and so when he took effort to speak clearly, I could piece together what he was saying.]

On the way home, I stopped at the Elephant Pharmacy to get the prescription filled. This seemed to go smoothly (though I didn't hear them page me as I waited). There was, however, a problem: it turns out that the drug that the clinic prescribed has a potential for severe interactions with another medication that I'm taking, interactions that the pharmacist called "nasty and cardiovascular." They'll be calling the clinic then calling me. Unless things clear up a bit by morning, I probably won't be able to take the call. But when I feel the phone ring (the vibrate setting is so useful) and see that they've called, I'll walk down there and see what's up.

But that's it for now, a torrent of words perhaps trying to fill the space of those that I can't hear. This has all been so amazingly absurd that I've been approaching it with somewhat more of a sense of bemused wonderment than of annoyance. That whatever stroke of weird chance this is has attacked my ability to hear both music and human speech is so patently wacky and so directly hits my areas of skill and pride (is Job on the job again?) that I would figure it for bad scriptwriting if I were to encounter in a film based on me. But then, sometimes a keen taste for the ridiculous is a sort of survival instinct.

The Fog That Shrouds the Horns

5 April 2005

Well, here it is a week later. About half of my hearing seems to have returned. The sound within my head remains, quieter now, but still present. According to my pitch pipe, the primary note is about a D natural above middle C. The other pitches that appear are within a major third above and below, the notes farther away from it less frequent that the ones near it. Interestingly, I don't hear beats forming when notes close to one another sound. I don't know what this tells me about the problem. And the shimmering cloud of noise drifts behind the pitches, forming a backing haze to whatever I hear from outside myself.

I still have trouble understanding voices that are more than a few feet from me unless they are spoken quite clearly. I can understand some pages over the speaker system at work, but not others. High-pitched or somewhat nasal voices work best. Deeper or mellower voices are much more difficult, meaning that I can barely understand a few of my dulcet-toned, soft spoken coworkers at all.

I'm doing better at understanding customers, though it takes hard work. I'm not engaging with customers at a distance to the extent that I'd like, and sometimes have to ask them a few times to clarify what they want. It's most difficult with people looking for classical music, especially if they are native speakers of a language or dialect other than North American English looking for a composer or performer whose names were in yet another language. I had to give up today on a customer who was looking for the opera *blur* conducted by *mumble*, but not the recording from *smear.*

I can differentiate music more readily, but have to concentrate quite hard to get a real sense of it. Music with which I'm already familiar seems clearer, but that's probably my memory filling in the gaps. Some unfamiliar music disappears completely—today we played what seems like a promising album by Lea DeLaria, but by the end I could only recall having heard two songs. And music below a certain volume disappears in the noise; I've had to ask coworkers whether classical CDs that I was playing (which have greater differences in dynamic range than discs in most other genres) had ended.

I'm also getting better at faking whether I heard something completely and at figuring out what was meant, though that's hard work. I don't think I've made too many egregious errors. And my coworkers have been good at compensating for and putting up with the problem, as well as occasionally gently ribbing me about it.

(The conversations that I do hear seem to be getting odder. While I'm used to some explicit conversations among the workers, and sometimes dismayed at the extent to which some swear within earshot of customers, some of what I hear is even beyond what I expect. A few days ago, I came upon a group of huddled coworkers, one of whom seemed to be diagramming something in the air with his hands, as he said, "Well, it lifts it up at a better angle, so there's deeper penetration and better contact between their—uh, hi, Joe. We were just talking about, uh, upselling the new Bright Eyes album."

"Better market penetration?" I asked. They nodded. Some blushed.)

I can also now understand most of the dialog on TV shows played on my PC, where the speakers are fairly nearby. Watching the Common Room TV is still frustrating. And I can hear things quite well on headphones, including those on my MP3 player.

When the pharmacist at Elephant Pharmacy spotted the danger of interactions with what the doctor had prescribed, he promised to call the doctor the next day and get some clarification and a replacement prescription. I came back to the pharmacy at close to 5 PM the next day, and he said that they hadn't heard back from the doctor yet. I wandered off, frustrated.

Once I was outside, though, and headed away from the store rather briskly, I felt a tap on my shoulder. Turning around, I saw the pharmacist, who had run to catch up with me. The doctor had just called back, and given them a replacement prescription for Flonase, a nasal decongestant. (Unlike the previous prescription, it doesn't go through the bloodstream, and thus avoids some problems.) They had tried to page me, and he had called my name as he approached me, but I hadn't heard. By the time he caught up with me and brought me back to the pharmacy counter, the prescription was already filled and ready.

That's really amazing customer service, and gets them a lot of repeat business. I often shop there for things that I could probably find less expensively a couple of blocks away, but it's worth giving these folks my business.

As I was sitting at home, bored, last Tuesday, unable to sleep, listen to music, or watch TV, I started to think about the problem that some of our customers have in finding classical CDs. We have some discs classified by composer and some by performer, with the difference between the categories often being quite obscure. I got an idea for a way to create cards that would direct customers from artists' bins to the other places that the artists would be found. Thinking led to sketching, sketching led to data retrieval, data retrieval led to tweaking the data, which led to coming up with file formats, graphic design, and the like, with much backtracking and rethinking of earlier steps, and after about eight hours, I had something to present as a solution.

I presented a set of the cards, with explanation, to my management tree. (Due to the weird lining up of schedules, my direct supervisor saw it last. But though my higher-ups were eager to run with it, I tried to make sure that he saw and approved it before we took any action, so it wouldn't seem as if I had routed the decision around him.) They all flipped, and it looks like we're going with a prototype. I'm hoping that we can send this up the chain and see if it can eventually be used in our other stores.

My supervisor, looking at the result, said that I really should be working at corporate headquarters. We daydreamed that my perfect job would be as the company's "MacGyver," going from store to store, talking with the workers, seeing what could be improved in the stores, and doing small-scale things to help them and suggesting larger things. I think, though, that it would be important for me to continue working, at least part of the time, as a salesperson myself, so I would (as hacker jargon has it) eat my own dog food, experiencing the results first hand. Too many bad systems have been put into place by people coming up with, implementing, and changing systems without getting direct feedback on how they work.

The Fabric of Customer Days

23 May 2005

I had an interesting language glitch today at work. When a customer brought some items that she wanted to purchase to the information desk, I told her that we didn't have any registers there, but that she could bring them to the registers on the ground floor. She looked at me oddly. "I have to register to buy things here?"

While I try to be on the lookout for using jargon with people who wouldn't follow it, this one had gotten past me: I had unconsciously used the term "registers" as short for "cash registers," something that most workers at the store would understand, but few others. And this was not long after I had reminded another worker that her page for a customer to come to "Info One" probably wouldn't work, since few would understand that to mean the information desk on the first floor.

Chapter 19

This has actually been quite a weekend for odd communications. Last night, I was driven nearly nuts (OK, more nuts) by a customer trying to find a piece by Schubert that she'd heard on the radio. She insisted that the name of the piece was "Number Two," and she couldn't recall if it was for orchestra, voices, solo instruments, or anything else. The best that I could do was to guide her to the catalog of compositions and show her the large number of "Number Two" pieces that Schubert had written.

Another customer recently, when I asked if I could help, grimaced and said, "I'm afraid not. You don't have Martha doing the G Major."

Fortunately, since he was at the Piano collections, I knew that he meant Martha Argerich, and he was finally willing to tell me that he was looking for Ravel. I found that our database (which is often prone to hallucinatory optimism) claimed that we had one recording of Argerich doing the piece, but I wasn't able to find it. . . until several hours later, when the disc appeared several rows away, where someone had plopped it down among the Prokofiev.

One Japanese customer today asked me, with lots of unintelligible hand gestures, if we had "kosobishu". I eventually figured out that she meant DVDs of The Cosby Show.

Another customer, late in the evening, exhibited some of the strangest speech patterns that I had ever heard, in looking for DVDs of Jerry Lewis movies. It turns out, as he told us proudly, that he was from Tokyo, and had taught himself English by sneaking into those movies repeatedly when he was a teenager. Another worker was able to identify an Elvis Presley song that the customer had recalled as "I Am Searching For Your Dreams" as "Follow That Dream." The customer got a lot of stuff, but maximized the absurdity when, in the course of the transaction, he paused to unzip and drop his pants, adjust his underwear, then refasten his clothes.

I had a sadder case a few days ago. A very old gentleman, after looking for some Stan Kenton (which we had) asked me if we had any music by Howard Rumsey. I looked, and saw that we didn't have any, but could order some. He declined, and wandered off.

A few minutes later, he came back, and said, "I had meant to ask you about another artist. Might you have any records by Howard Rumsey?" I raised an eyebrow, but looked again, much more quickly, and told him, again, that we didn't have any, but could order some.

And again, a few minutes after that, he returned to the information desk. "By the way, have you heard of an artist named Howard Rumsey?"

"Funny you should ask that," I said. "I hadn't heard of him before today, but a customer was in here earlier this evening asking about him. Unfortunately, we don't have any of his albums, but can order some." He thanked me profusely, since he said that he hadn't met anyone in a record store who had ever heard of him. And then his wife showed up with her purchases and guided him out of the store.

The Walrus and the Party! Disc

20 May 2005

The family came up the escalator just as I was about to head to lunch.

Three young girls, one boy, and four adults (parents and grandparents, I think) clustered together when they all reached our floor. They glanced about anxiously, as if afraid to be in a store this large.

"Can I help you find anything?" I asked.

The younger man pointed to one of the girls. "She wants Jesse McCartney."

"Yes," she said. "Where is Jesse McCartney?"

"Follow me," I said, and started toward our Pop/Rock section. The family trailed behind me, the youngest girl trotting forward to walk by my side. While I had begun to walk at my usual pace, faster than most others can move (for a big guy, I'm pretty quick and light on my feet), I throttled back to my usual walking-with-customers mode: when I only move my legs from the knees down, it's slow enough for others to keep up. "He's over here, just before Paul."

"Who is Paul?" one of the children asked.

"He was a walrus," I replied.

"OK!" said the youngest, who now was swinging her arms as she walked, the stuffed animal that she was carrying (either Kanga or Roo) bumping repeatedly against my shin. One of the grownups chuckled. I don't think the others got it.

When we got to the right bin, I fished the Jesse McCartney disc out with a flourish, and handed it to the girl who had asked for it. She clutched it to her chest and yelled, "Yes!"

The boy rolled his eyes and whined, "What do I get?" The parents thanked me and I wandered back to the information desk. The family quickly dispersed around the sales floor.

After a while, I saw the youngest girl standing to one side of my desk, scanning up and around. "Can I help you find anything?" I asked again.

"Do you have another one of those things my sister's using?"

I looked around and spotted the older girl looking up information at one of our information kiosks. "You can use this computer here," I said, pointing at the PC that faced outward from my information desk.

"Oh," she said, looking up at it and frowning. The surface on which the keyboard and mouse rested were well above her reach, and the screen was out of her sight.

I searched until I found a step stool that she could use. I brought it to her, and she stepped up on it.

She looked at the screen and moved the mouse around.

"Do you know how to use this?" I asked.

"I know how to click things." she replied.

"Well, I can show you how to use it," I said. I came around and stood behind her, one hand on the keyboard and the other guiding her tiny, soft hand on the mouse. "What music do you like to listen to?"

"I like Lizzie McGuire," she said.

"OK," I said. I guided the mouse to the Music button, "We click here," and then to the Title selector, "and then here," and then to the text entry field, "and then here, and we put the name here."

She leaned forward and stared at the screen. "How?" she asked. Looking up and then around at me, she lost her balance on the step stool and tilted backward with a sudden "Oh!," her weight resting back against me.

I reached between us, placed one hand between her shoulders and one behind the small of her back, and lifted her forward, supporting her until she was again certain of her balance.

I moved my hands back to the keyboard and mouse, typed "lizzie," and then paused. "Um, I'm not sure how to spell 'McGuire'. Do you know?"

"Nope!" she answered brightly. "I don't know how to read yet."

"Hmm," I said, not having realized that.

I heard a laugh behind me, a little to my left, and turned to see her father standing there grinning, one hand already carrying several CDs.

"Just try it with 'lizzie'," he said. "That should bring it up OK."

He was right. Most of the items that showed up on the first page of results were indeed for Lizzie McGuire. We had several albums related to the TV show and one from the movie in stock. "It's in Kids Music, over here." I gestured toward the section.

The girl hopped off the step stool and ran off, almost in the right direction but down the wrong aisle. "Hold on," I called, "I'll show you." Her father nodded at me and remained at the information desk as the third sister began to ask him about something.

I caught up with the girl near the end of the aisle. "Follow me," I said. She ran to my right as I headed around the pillar at the end and over to Kids Music. The movie album was there in the Soundtracks area. I handed it to her.

"Good!" she said. "Are there more?"

I looked near it, but didn't see any. "There should be more," I said. "I'll ask the computer for more information."

I walked back to the screen, took a closer look, and returned.

"They're in with the other Disney discs," I said. Looking through the Disney section of the Kids bin, I found one other, the *Total Party!* CD, and handed it to her too. It took a bit of juggling and handing items back and forth before she figured out how to hold both CDs and her stuffed animal at the same time.

She ran back to her father. I followed close behind. "Look what I found!" she said, handing them to him.

Her brother grabbed them, glanced at them, then shoved them back at me. "We have them already," he said.

"Are you sure?" the father asked.

"Yeah, yeah," he replied. "The movie CD, *Total Party!*, everything. She has everything Lizzie McGuire there is. We don't want them."

"Do we already have them?" the father asked the girl. She didn't answer, but sat down glumly on the step stool, her face buried in the stuffed animal.

"Do we already have them?" he repeated. I heard a quiet, muffled "Uh-huh" from the girl. "Then we shouldn't get them again," he said.

The girl looked up. "But I want them!" she wailed.

"Maybe we can get you something else," he said. "It's only four o'clock, and we have more stores to go to."

"Hey!" her brother yelled, having wandered a few aisles over but still within earshot. "Why do we have to keep getting her things?"

The father looked at the boy, then at the girl, then at me. "Thank you," he said. He leaned over and put his hand on the girl's shoulder. "Say thank you to the man."

The girl murmured something that I took to be another "Thank you."

"You're welcome," I said, and stepped away.

A moment later, as I stood by the Soundtracks area, the girl came trotting up to me again, her family following behind her. "I have to put these back," she said.

"OK," I said, stepping a few feet over to the Kids Music. "Do you remember where they were?"

"Yes," she said. She reached up, pushed forward the CDs that were in front of the place for the *Total Party!* CD and easily put it back. Then standing on her toes and stretching out her arm, she almost reached the place for the movie soundtrack.

"That's OK," I said, and reached for the CD.

"No," she said adamantly. "*I* have to put it back."

Her father knelt down, put his hands under her arms, and lifted her up and forward until she was able to reach the right spot. The girl turned within his grasp and put her arms around his neck, the stuffed animal bouncing against the back of his head. He shifted his hands so that they supported her, and stood, holding her so that she rested in his arms, her head against his shoulder.

"Goodbye," I said.

"Bye," her father said. "Thanks again." He headed off to the checkout line, his family following him, the boy once again badgering him, this time for a light saber. I went back to the information desk, retrieved my coffee cup, and finally headed off to lunch.

CHAPTER 20

After the Dreaded Phone Call

18 November 2005

My father passed away this morning at 6:05 AM in New Jersey.
I'm flying out there in a few hours, for at least 10 days.
I will have my cell phone with me.

A Letter to My Father

14 December 2005

Dear Aba:

Your funeral went well. As you'd asked, it was a combination of a religious and a military ceremony. I understand that you were buried in your tallit and army jacket (though, since your plain pine casket was closed, I didn't see you for myself). The weather was

195

perfect. I don't know if any day could be a good day for a funeral, but this was as close as it gets.

My brother and I had come to your house the previous day, leaving our mother's house as soon as I arrived from the airport. Your wife was off at the cemetery, making arrangements. Since messages got scrambled while we were there, we left before she returned, heading back to our mothers'. We stopped for a while for dinner before we got there.

Remembering that you had introduced us to sushi, we went to the sushi buffet not far from you for a sort of dinner in your memory.

The next morning, we made the long drive from the Jersey shore to the cemetery on Long Island. Since we had allowed for plenty of "getting lost time," we got there quite early, stopping off at a diner a few miles past the site for a sandwich and some coffee before we went to the cemetery itself.

When we arrived at the cemetery, we parked at the main building and went in to see what to do next. We had been told that, as your sons, my brother and I would have to identify your body officially before the ceremony could begin. No one at the desk knew what that might have been about, and we were told to "just hang out in front" until someone official arrived.

There were several funeral parties shuffling in and out, and it was twenty minutes or so before we recognized anyone: first our cousin Elliott on your side, then our other cousin Elliott on your wife's side, then his father, and then the Rabbi. The Rabbi wasn't quite sure where to go either, but he said that the funeral director would answer all questions when he arrived.

After a brief delay, the hearse pulled up on the main road. It had taken a detour from where your body had been (a funeral home? the hospital?) to the cemetery: your wife had promised you that you would come home from the hospital, so she asked that the hearse drive you past your house one last time.

Those of us who were out front of the main building piled back into our cars and followed the hearse to the grave site. When the chain of traffic stopped, we all parked, got out, and walked the rest of the way. At the entrance to the family plot, a man in uniform stood perfectly still, eyes focused straight ahead, clutching a bugle.

We gathered at the grave site, where your casket rested on braces above the deep grave that had already been dug and neatened up. An American flag was draped over the casket, perfectly arrayed. Canvas straps extended out from under the casket to its left and right. (I understand that you had wanted an Israeli flag too, but that American military protocol had prevented it.) A tall mound of dirt rested nearby, with a shovel sticking up into the air.

The crowd of several dozen arrayed itself on the grass facing the casket as the funeral director handed out kippot. Your wife, of course, stood front and center, with her children and grandchildren arrayed around her. My brother and I made our way to the front, off to their right. The others (most of whom I didn't recognize) fanned out behind us.

Two more soldiers stood in front of the mound. At a signal from the funeral director, one barked an order that I didn't understand, and the other came to his side as they snapped to attention.

From far behind us, where the other soldier stood, came the sound of Taps, played slowly and clearly on his bugle. A few notes in, the sound of an approaching plane began, starting a couple of steps under the tonic of the key in which the bugle played, and steadily sliding up in pitch, passing overhead and finally fading out, just as Taps ended, about a fifth above the note on which it began.

In the following silence, the two soldiers in front of us moved to the ends of the casket, lifted the flag, and, in precise, mechanical movements, folded the flag into a triangle, almost perfect. (The soundscape was a symphony of sniffles from the many people surrounding us who were crying.) The one who had given the order at the beginning lifted the flag, tucked in some edges to finish the exact maneuver, then walked forward, stopping in front of your wife.

He bent down to look her directly in the eyes. With a gaze and voice of infinite gentleness and kindness, he said something like "On behalf of the President of the United States and a grateful nation, please accept this flag as a symbol of our appreciation for your loved one's honorable and faithful service." (Your wife later admitted that, in any other circumstance, she would have said something biting at the mention of our current President.)

That's when I finally started crying, quietly, as, I think, did my brother. Whether the soldier's demeanor was genuine or merely perfectly rehearsed, it had brought the first moment of emotion to an abstract event.

The Rabbi took over at that point, saying the appropriate prayers, and delivering a moving remembrance of you. (At one point in the eulogy, his cell phone went off, but he silenced it with good humor and continued.) He spoke of your long friendship, first down in South Jersey when you were married to our mother, then up in North Jersey, where he was at your latter wife's synagogue when you joined her there. He spoke of your activity in the congregation, participating in your joint sermon/debates, taking your Torah courses and helping with them, and being a fountain of knowledge on demand. He did allude to the clash that drove you apart for much of your last few years, but spoke of being with you again on your final day.

But mostly, he spoke of the experiences that you had of which you were the most proud: the work in the military in World War II, both on the Stars and Stripes newspaper and as a navigator with the Air Force (and here I had thought, for some reason, that you were in the Army and stationed on the ground), your efforts in Machal working to pull together an army for Israel just before the state began, and your never-ending task of educating later generations about the Holocaust.

(A prominent Rabbi who visited our sister in Israel as she was sitting shiva last week said that for these activities, you have certainly been accepted directly into heaven.)

After the eulogy, the Rabbi read more prayers and psalms (and when he hit the line about the "table before my enemies" in Psalm 23, I couldn't help but picture a comic-strip thought balloon appearing above your casket saying, as you always insisted, "That line's a mistake— there's a typo in the Hebrew.") He then attached small black ribbons to your wife's, my brother's, and my lapels, and ripped each, the sound of the tearing of the ribbons said to symbolize the tearing of our hearts at your passing. We said Kaddish with him; even though I have never had occasion before to speak the Mourner's Kaddish, I found that I had the words, cadences, and rhythms already memorized.

The gravediggers, who had been standing by reverently throughout the service, came forward and, lifting the canvas straps that lay under the casket. lowered it evenly to the bottom of the grave. The Rabbi then stepped over to the mound of earth, removed the shovel, and dropped several scoops of the dry dirt onto your casket. My brother and I did likewise; I only dropped a single shovelful down (the grains and clumps sounding a chaotic snare-roll on the resonant pine), but my brother dropped several, standing, as he said, for his children and for our sister and her children who could not be there themselves.

Looking around as the crowd dispersed, I looked at the gravestones of your wife's family, including the newest, that of her sister who passed away almost exactly a year before you. I visualized your grave as it would come to be, filled in, covered with lush grass, the gravestone bearing your full Hebrew name (if Tzvi Hirsch ben Micha Yosef would fit). I wondered if they'll put on it the epitaph that you had said that you wanted: "I have a book about that. . . "

And then we went back to our cars, leaving in the order in which we had parked. Most of us headed back to your house, though the caravan quickly became scattered, and we had to find our way back without following anyone. The directions that we had printed out from one of the Internet map sites were pretty good, though one turn faked us out and led us to a dead end. Once nearer your house, I was able to remember some of the way there ("Turn right at this Dunkin' Donuts, follow this road as it squiggles around, and take the first left after this other Dunkin' Donuts"), and we made it to the house without too much hassle.

We were somewhat nervous about what we were supposed to be doing, on our first experience as mourners to whom people were making a shiva call. But the Rabbi had said that there is no "supposed to," only what would feel right for us. Outside the front door there was, as traditional, a container of water and a basin into which we could pour the water over our hands, ceremonially washing them. We did so, and went in.

The house was full of people, some of whom we knew, some of whom we didn't, and some whose identities we figured out after not having seen them in many years. My brother, his friend who came to the funeral with us, and I mostly hovered on the periphery. Occasionally people came up to us to express brief condolences, and we got to talk to a few people we recognized or thought that we did. I spent a while talking with a cousin's son, sharing our tales of each trying to set up your computers.

Much of what people told us consisted of stories about how great you were with the second family's kids, as step-grandfather or more remotely related family elder. It seems that you were a wonderful grandfather, even to family members whom I didn't even know existed. My brother (whose image of you is, of course, flavored by having grown up living with my mother, with you relatively far away) bristled with ever-increasing resentment at how you were there for them when you were not there for him.

The Rabbi returned in the evening, assembled a minyan of us, and led an evening service (from a prayer book that, among other things, made the conceptual organization of the eighteen prayers in the Amidah clearer than I had ever seen before). He, your wife, my brother and I said Kaddish again, and the Rabbi directed some comforting comments directly to us.

My mother did make an effort to let me sit shiva somewhat traditionally at her house, offering to cover the mirrors and to invite her synagogue's standing minyan over so that I could say Kaddish for you, and digging out the one yahrzeit candle that she had in the house. But it didn't feel right, since she wasn't mourning, and her living room was in continual use as her teaching studio, so I declined.

I got to spend some good time with my niece and nephew. My brother had been worried about how to tell them that you had passed away, but they seemed to take it well. The last time I saw them was Passover of last year, long enough ago for his daughter not to remember me, though I used to see them several times a week some years ago.

(Writing this, I suddenly flashed on my first memory of you. Sometime in 1963, when I was four or five, we had moved from Winnipeg to New Jersey, with you going on ahead of us to start work. I was sitting watching TV in my grandmother's living room when you walked in. I don't remember your face from back then, but I do recall your shape, silhouetted in the afternoon sun coming through the front bay windows, and your white t-shirt and black trousers. I asked who you were, and you said you were my father. I think I nodded and went back to watching TV.)

On Sunday, as we all headed to a nearby skating rink, my niece looked up at me quizzically again and asked, "Are you my uncle?"

"Yes," I said again.

"Are you Uncle Jack?"

"No, but I have an Uncle Jack."

"Yeah," the boy chimed in, "but he's old. like ninety."

"Uncle Jack is ninety five," my mother said.

"That's old," he said again.

"Pop-pop's old, too," the girl said, speaking of you.

"Yeah," said the boy. "But he's dead."

"He's dead," the girl repeated. "So he's everywhere now, like God."

"Yeah, like God."

In my mother's basement, my brother ran across the photo album from your wedding to my mother, over fifty years ago. It's amazing to see how young you looked then, in your late twenties, your eyes and face echoing those of all the men on your side of the family. I scanned in some of the pictures, and emailed them to myself for safekeeping.

Back in California, I have found a tape that you made for your granddaughter, some twenty years ago, when she was seven years old. On the tape, you spoke for close to half an hour about your experiences as an American soldier and correspondent liberating the Nazi death camps during and after World War II. As I dubbed the tape to the computer, cleaned up the sound, and uploaded it to the Internet Archive where anyone can now hear it, I was struck by the clarity and power of your voice.

The voice that I mostly have in my memory of you is that of your final three years, when your stroke in the hospital (after the heart failure, before they found the cancer) audibly changed your speech patterns, making your voice less clear and much higher in pitch. Since I wasn't around much, I didn't really realize how much the stroke had affected you until the Rabbi talked about it at and after the funeral.

It's good to recall that you didn't always sound lost, frightened, and overwhelmed. On this tape, you speak clearly, directly, and effectively, telling of your perceptions and experiences with the cadences of a skilled speaker and teacher. And the passion comes through in your voice, insisting that no one ever again must forget or deny the horrors that you saw and the evil that created them. And you offered hope that your granddaughter, in growing up, would understand more and more of what you said on the tape, and carry your legacy forward. (As it turns out, she had lost her copy of the tape years ago, and was overjoyed when she learned that I had made and kept a backup and uploaded it to where it should stay available in perpetuity.)

It's several weeks later now, and I'm back to work as usual (if anything in retail in December can be called "usual"). I've gotten a lot of support and condolences from friends and coworkers, in words and embraces, in cards, by email, and by responses to my post about your passing in my blog. I haven't been back to synagogue to say Kaddish for you (though I understand that my Orthodox brother-in-law is doing so consistently) or followed much of the other traditions, which feel somewhat out of context.

I did buy a set of yahrzeit candles (finding them at the local Safeway supermarket, hidden behind boxes of latke mix), and have been burning them in my room. They're supposed to burn for 24 hours each, but (especially in light of my menorah fire last Chanukah) it isn't safe to leave anything burning unattended here, so I'm lighting them when I'm awake and in my room for an extended time.

I do think of you several times each day, reminded by small things. And I did have an odd moment at work a few days ago, when doing my holiday shopping. Spotting a wonderful book on synagogue architecture, I took it off the shelf and put it in my basket, thinking that it would be a great Chanukah present for you. But then I remembered that I won't be able to give objects to you ever again, sighed, and put it back.

I don't particularly believe in an afterlife, though I like how my niece described you as being "everywhere." Yet I still find myself writing this as if you might read it, and engaging in other tiny fictions to keep myself and others going in your absence. But I'm told that my brother and sister, their children, those who you influenced in your second family, and I are your legacy, as are your words that are now online.

So sleep well, drift about amiably, or dissipate in peace. We'll remember you.

Love,

Chapter 20

Joe
(or, as you used to call me, J. Throgmorton Flapdoodle. Or Butch.)

CHAPTER 21

Another Night in the Gauntlet

9 September 2006

Maybe it was the odd chill in the still-dry air; maybe it was that most of the crazed Europeans had run out of August days to spend here (though one family did get into a furious argument in Italian at my register as each tried to pay—one with a credit card, one with crumpled dollar bills, and one by dumping a small bag of change on the counter and trying to figure out the values of each coin in the mound —for one book; I stood, arms by my side, and waited, until the older man waved the charge card in the air in an odd gesture, inscrutable and possibly obscene, and got the other two to back down); maybe it was that the back-to-school materials were gone, and we were already getting memos about how earlier memos about the holiday schedule were wrong; but it was, quite ominously, beginning to feel a lot like Christmas.

The crowds in the store swarmed through in uneven bursts, never too much to handle, but never quite going away. The school year having started, the art books were getting pawed through and were strewn about by the students at the arts college, who then, not finding what they wanted, stormed over to us and demanded that we find for them the books that their teachers had assigned. When we told them that we were out of the books, they made it seem like we had committed a horrible faux pas; suggesting that they recommend to their professors that they let us know ahead of time what books they'd be assigning didn't help.

While I tried to help one regular customer figure out the name of a movie from the 80s that he vaguely remembered, another man stomped over, sun-burned and frazzle-haired, his Hawaiian shirt half in and half out of his shorts, and bellowed "Is anyone here to help customers, or are you just gabbing with this guy?"

The one to whom I was talking said "I'll be here for a while," and stepped back. The interrupter went into an extended spiel about how he was looking for CDs in a "Twenty Best Of" series, since he had gotten one of them a long time ago and had just seen in the liner notes that there were more. When I searched on our computers, I found that we did have two in the series, one of show tunes and one of Bluegrass Gospel. "Bluegrass Gospel!" he shouted. "That's what I want!"

We went over to the Bluegrass collections, and looked through them. He found the one he wanted, but then spotted two others. "Whoa, this one has thirty bluegrass gospels on two discs! And, no, wait, this one here has thirty on three discs for two bucks more? Is that gonna be two bucks better than the other one? Are they cramming the tunes on this one or stretching them on that one? You've heard them, right, which one sounds better? Or should I just stick with the twenty?"

I hadn't heard any of them, and knew very little of the genre. But I did get him to stop talking long enough to show him how to use the scan-and-play systems, so he could listen to excerpts of each on his own. I then went back to the first customer, and did, indeed manage to figure out the movie that he wanted. While we talked, I heard the Bluegrass Gospel guy occasionally yell out, "Whoa!" and "Yes, Lord!" from his listening station.

After a while, he came over to me, and said, "Man, I'm buying all of these!" He then leaned closer and said conspiratorially, "But I gotta tell ya, everyone here is strange! That guy over there keeps falling asleep, that guy with the black hat is just staring at people, and that one with the pants falling down is stomping around talking to himself. And that one over there smells to high heaven, and that lady, well, she doesn't smell bad really, but it's like some bar of flower soap exploded all over her. Y'all're just strange out here! But thank you for the records!"

As he lumbered off, I looked around at the other customers. He was right. There were a few unremarkable people around, but each of the others was as he described them.

By that point, the one with the pants falling down had landed in a chair near the DVDs, and was talking loudly enough to disturb the people near him. I wandered over to him, and picked up the two thick books of Kierkegaard that were on the ground next to the chair. "Are you still using these?" I asked.

He waved his hand as if dismissing them, stood up, and headed toward the escalator. "Naw, I'm done with all that. I'm going to the religion section, gonna pick myself out a god. You picked a god out yet?"

"Um, I think so," I mumbled as he stomped down to the next floor, still talking.

The rest of that hour was relatively sane. I helped a drummer from San Diego find some classic Afro-Cuban jazz ("Man, the stores down where I am got nothing! All those Mexicans around, you think they'd have the classic stuff, but nothing!"), and when we got to talk about rhythmic patterns, started explaining to him what I knew about the rhythmic structures in Bulgarian music. He got excited by it, and wanted to buy some, but our Eastern European section in World Music had been pretty much picked clean recently and hadn't yet been restocked. I did print out some suggestions for him, though, and told him that our San Diego stores could order anything that we did.

I spent the next hour on the ground floor, manning a cash register. There was a steady flow of customers making their purchases.

One man stomped up to me and said flatly, "You don't have any Israeli newspapers." I've learned that when people say that, they don't actually know if it's true, but think it puts them in some sort of stronger conversational stance than asking. "Well, I said, I'm pretty sure we carry *Haaretz* and *Yediot Achronot*. I'll see what we have."

We went over to the cubbyholes of newspapers behind the left end of the register counter. The customer, as so many do, stepped right over the barrier that's supposed to keep them away. "I see you have nothing," he said.

After I looked for a while, I did spot one, and picked it out for him. "Here's *Yediot*," I said. He grabbed it and handed it to an older woman who was following him. She glanced at it and slapped it back at me. "It's old. It's no good," she said. "I look at the headline and I see the news is already since a week old. Find a new one."

I shrugged. "That's what we have."

"So I find a good one somewhere?"

"Probably not at eleven at night. But since it's a week old, I'm guessing that we'll have the next one in a day or two."

"So. Maybe I am back then." She pivoted away, and stomped off with the other two.

None of the other customers were quite as grumpy. But it did take quite a bit of explaining to communicate to a couple from Romania why, due to the DVD region codes, the DVDs that they were getting might not play on their systems at home.

I did pretty well at signing customers up for our free discount cards. I have my spiel down to a line that I can deliver in a single breath, and most who don't already have the card willingly give me their email addresses.

One customer handed me her credit card and spewed a charming malapropism: "I am my first name, underscore, my last name, at dotmail hot com." I understood what she meant, and managed not to laugh.

As I was finishing the transaction, the Romanians returned, barging into the line and shoving the DVD that they had bought at me, nearly hitting the other customer. "I don't want this. But I get this. Maybe it works different at my home."

"OK," I said, "but I have to finish with this customer." I quickly unkeepered and bagged that customer's purchase, waited for her to leave, and turned back to the Romanians.

I looked at the new DVD. "Neither of these say if they have region codes. You'd be gambling with this one as much as with the other."

"OK," she said. "But you take this. I take that instead. It is the same price." She slammed the already-purchased DVD on the counter and stuffed the new one, with the security keeper still on it, in her bag.

"Wait!" I said. "I still have to officially exchange it."

"OK. Yes. OK," she said, looking put-upon. I rang up the return and purchase. Since they were, indeed, the same price, no money changed hands.

But when I looked down to hand her the receipt, I saw a credit card on the register keyboard. I picked it up, confused. "Is this yours?" I asked.

"No," she said, "I gave you no card now. It was the same price."

I looked more closely at the card. "Oh," I said, "this is bad. It's from the customer who was just here." I frantically looked around, and saw that she was gone. I then called the service manager, and told him of the forgotten card. He took it and put it in the safe.

It wasn't until I was walking home that I realized that I still remembered the email address of the person who had left the card. I'm usually oddly good at remembering the personal name parts of email addresses, but terrible at remembering, even for a moment, the domains, especially if they're from the Big Four (Gmail, Hotmail, Yahoo, or AOL). But since this customer had garbled the domain amusingly, I remembered it. When I got home, I emailed the Human Resources Manager, who I think will be the first one at the store in a few hours, told her the story, and asked her to email the customer to tell her that we have the card.

CHAPTER 22

No Sleep Till Bonynge

1 January 2007

They came up the escalator together: a very tall man, with grey hair and an expensive-looking coat, and a much smaller woman, also grey-haired, but with a coat that, if equally expensive, didn't seem designed to say anything about the wearer. When I asked them if I could help them find anything, they spoke simultaneously. I think she said something about Mozart operas; he, much more loudly, said, "No, we don't need anything. She's sleep-deprived."

Hearing the two speak at the same time short-circuited my linguistic handling (much like when I hear something over my headset when talking to a customer: what comes over the headset often doesn't even register as language), so I asked again. He sighed heavily and looked condescendingly at her as she asked if we had Mozart operas on CD.

I took them right over to the discs and asked which they wanted. I think she may have said something, but he jovially bellowed, "Oh, you know, the usual top four." I pointed out recordings of *The Magic Flute, Don Giovanni, La Clemenza de Tito, Cosi Fan Tutte,* and *Zaide.* The woman picked up the *Don Giovanni,* but the man said, "No, you already have this," then, to me, "I'm sorry, she's sleep-deprived."

She scowled at him. "We have highlights of *Don Giovanni.* This is the whole thing." He took it from her, glanced at it, and chucked it back down in the bin. "This looks cheap. None of these are the major singers." It actually was cheap, and probably a lousy item, since it was one of those tacky packagings of European broadcasts that have come out of copyright. But, from what I recall, at least one of the singers was a known star.

"I think we have more," I said, and brought them to the locked cases.

"Oh,," he said, "so this is where you hide the good stuff."

"Well, what's in here tends to be more expensive, but it's a bit arbitrary. Almost all our Mahler that isn't in jewel cases is in here, for example, since that gets stolen a lot if it isn't." I unlocked the lower case and pulled out one box. "Here's a good *Don Giovanni.*"

"Why is it this only $35? It can't be that good."

"It's an EMI reissue, and from what I can tell, it should be good."

"I don't know these names," he snorted.

"Well, Bernard Haitink's reputable as a conductor, and Thomas Allen should be a good Giovanni."

"So you're, like, the classical genius around here."

"Well, it's my section."

"So I wouldn't ask you any weird rock and roll questions, then."

"Actually, I'd probably be able to handle those, too. But officially, I'm the classical guy."

"So if I were to ask you what's the absolute best *Don Giovanni,* what would you say?"

"Well, I'm kind of an atypical classical guy. I pretty much like everything. I can show you the guides to classical recordings, each of which might have suggestions."

"So what's the absolute best record guide?"

"Penguin's quite good. I tend to check the Gramophone guide first, and the NPR and All Music guides are good, too. Once you have dealt with them awhile, you'll start to get a sense of which match your tastes."

"So they have online sites to look things up." He said this as a statement, not a question.

"They might, but for these, the books are the way to go. I can show you where they are—"

"So if I google for Gramophone, it will give me their book online."

"I don't know—"

"Then the, what was it, the Penguin is there."

"If you're going to check online, the one sure thing is the All-Music Guide, though they tend to be kind of negative and cranky about things."

The woman spoke up. "Yes, where are those books?"

"Sorry," the man said. "She's sleep-deprived. So where are they online? We're with the UN, and we're here for a week and a half, and we have high-speed broadband."

"The All Music Guide is online, though I'm not exactly sure of the URL. I think it's allmusic.com, but googling on All Music Guide should find it."

"So that's the best guide online."

I shrugged. "It's a good guide."

"Where are the architecture books?" the woman asked.

"We're going back to the hotel," he said. "She's sleep-deprived. UN, you know."

"Well, to some of us it feels like jet lag is a lifestyle," I said.

"This is serious jet lag. I'm on Kabul time. She's on Kosovo time. Sleep-deprived. We're going back to the hotel. We'll look things up online and we'll be sure to come back and buy things here."

He took her by the hand and led her toward the escalator. Apparently, she won out, though, for a while; I saw them a few minutes later in the architecture section, where she was looking at a small book (possibly *A Pattern Language*) while he flipped through a larger photo book. When I went back to that section at the end of the night, her book was neatly back in place, while his was dumped, still open and threatening to slide to the floor, on top of a messy stack of similar books.

I sighed and put the books back on the shelf. There's little else to do with them, and no way to argue effectively with the customers. Especially when the schedules have us so sleep-deprived.

CHAPTER **23**

The Naming of Customers

6 January 2007

As closing time approached, I went around the music floor to make sure all of the customers had left. One that I had seen earlier didn't seem to be around, though I hadn't seen him leave. "Is Tracksuit Man still here?" I asked Material Girl.

A voice came from the far side of a bookshelf. "Yes, I am."

Oops.

We haven't learned the names of a lot of the regular customers and denizens at the store. Some have acquired names as we talk about them, though few of them know what they're called. (I make an effort to learn the real names of some customers, but not all are that approachable.)

Tracksuit Man comes in almost every night in the last half hour that we're open, always dressed in a sharp-looking blue tracksuit and carrying a satchel about the size of a rolled up yoga mat. He quickly and silently strides to the back of the floor, where he sits in one of our comfortable black chairs with an art book. A few minutes before we close, he gets up, reshelves the book where he got it, and strides out as he came in. His eyes always seem fixed on a specific item (though not quite staring), either down at his book or straight ahead, with a stern impassiveness.

There was a lot of chatter over the headsets today about people in the store. One regular, who has been dubbed Rico Suave, tends to hang out in the café and try to pick up women. He arrived with a woman today, and left without her, though the talk was that he had tried to pick up someone else while she was there, which displeased her.

Other people were reported sleeping in the store, causing major messes in the café and elsewhere, and being particularly tenacious in buttonholing several workers in a row with desperate quests for nonexistent items. In the latter cases, the headsets came in quite handy, as workers were able to warn the customer's next target to disengage quickly or to duck before he saw them.

Of the characters who frequent the store, I deal with Thumper (who listens to the same 30-second excerpts from the same soundtrack CDs every night, often stamping his foot in rhythm), Chess Guy (who used to come in with a large chess board, set it up on a table, then lounge in a comfortable chair quite far away, though he would pounce upon and harass anyone else who tried to sit near his chess board), and Miss Giggles (who comes in and talks and laughs to herself, often leaving a trail of Bibles where she's been) quite frequently. I hear talk on the headsets about The Senator, Moto, The Captain and Tennille, and others, but I often haven't seen them, since they haven't discovered the way up to the music floor.

I often realize, after a while, that a former denizen has gone away, and I find myself wondering what became of him. I remembered today, while reshelving a book on Ray Harryhausen, that it had been months since I'd seen one particular customer, who seemed intellectually challenged and would build and carry around plaster models of mythical monsters and creatures from old movies.

Another man would come in looking for music with which he might connect with his son, who was living on the streets and was a fan of the band Fenix TX. The man seemed determined to do whatever he could for his son —but I've recently seen them both, after a long time out of sight, at the all-night Jack In The Box a few blocks from work, neither looking as if he had slept or bathed in days.

Yet another (one of two people who were dubbed Guitar Guy, which got confusing) would come in with an acoustic guitar without a case and write down bits of music from our score books, longhand on manuscript paper. He had been seen on the streets playing his guitar while asking for change, though he hadn't quite gotten to some of the fine points of playing the guitar, such as tuning it. (Come to think of it, the other Guitar Guy might have been the same as Chess Guy, but I've lost track.)

We seemed to have far fewer of these people around during the Christmas craziness, though their presence may just have been drowned out by the crowds. But with the mobs having abated, they are slowly making their way back in.

Tracksuit Man did seem amused, in a sort of deadpan way, that he had been noticed and named. When I said "Good night" to him as he left tonight, he nodded slightly toward me. I think he almost smiled.

In the Media Ward

29 January 2007

The music that blasts from the children's shop next door to and below ours often gets stuck in my head, bursting back into my consciousness when least welcome. Today, it was playing the original "Someday My Prince Will Come," Adriana Caselotti's implausible vibrato slicing through the grinding groan of frustrated traffic and the half conversations of crowded, isolated people, only some of whom had telephones. On Saturday, it was the impossibly cheerful music of an imagined old world, a sort of Chipmunk Klezmer of the Damned.

I got to the store a little earlier than needed today, the BART gods having been unusually merciful in their timing for a Sunday. I had time to hunt down my coffee cup and stop through the café on the second floor on my way up to my post.

As often happens, the line at the café had forked, with some people queued up toward the business books and more standing alongside the pastry case. The lines merged pretty amicably, with a rough alternation of people taking their places. The person in the spot corresponding to mine in the other fork, however, continually made it clear that he was to be handled before me, stamping his feet and stretching out his arms, pretending that he didn't see me. I think I annoyed him somewhat by not challenging his position, making his gestures seem even more pointless and lame.

When I finally got to the front of the line, I handed my coffee cup to Meriadoc. "Just coffee, Joe?"

"Yup," I said. "Nectar of the geeks."

"No, that's Mountain Dew. We're out of that. So, coffee. Do you want Seattle's Best blend or the Saturday's blend?"

"Saturday's blend? On a Sunday?"

Meriadoc shrugged. "It's about as much sense as drinking Seattle's Best in San Francisco."

"I like the logic. I'll go for the Saturday's blend."

Meriadoc poured a cup, the last bit of it dripping reluctantly from the spout. "Looks like that's the last of it. Maybe it *was* from yesterday."

"Should be good and strong, then. I like coffee I can chew."

The fourth floor was relatively quiet when I got up there. A few customers milled around, trying to decide on purchases or just enjoying their shopping meditations. With the "Buy 3, get a 4th free" sale on DVDs ending today, several were wandering with three that that really wanted, daunted by the prospect of finding a fourth.

One looked relieved when I asked if I could help her. "I hear that *Bambi* and *Lady and the Tramp I & II* are going to be disappearing soon. Where are they?"

I guided her to the Disney shelves. "Disney's like that. They release DVDs for a few months, then pull them off the shelves for several years. I think they took *Sleeping Beauty* too literally." I spotted the three discs, pulled them, and handed them to her.

"But what do I get for a fourth disc?" she asked.

"*Bambi's Revenge?*" I suggested.

"Bambi's back!" she said in a mock-announcer's voice. "And he's got his therapist with him!"

(There actually was a *Bambi II*, but I understand that it wasn't particularly traumatic. And then there was *Bambi Meets Godzilla*... which apparently was made at a studio owned by Adriana Cascolotti... which shows that almost any random chain of references might converge somewhere...)

We had the usual array of Manga teens lounging about, leaving their trails of read magazines and graphic novels lying on the floor and on windowsills. Other teenagers sat on the floor in various aisles, acting as if they had marked off their own personal phone booths, and looking annoyed when people came near them or stepped over them, interrupting their conversations. Grownups with cell phones prowled the rest of the floor, darting away as others approached, looking as if rude people had barged into their offices.

One tiny girl, maybe two years old, with long brown hair and high boots more stylish that one might expect to see on someone so small, ran laps around the entire floor. She didn't seem to be related to any grownups that I could see, and repeatedly barely missed crashing into people and other objects.

Most of the times that she ran past, I was engaged with other customers, so I couldn't intervene. After several circuits, though, I was able to step out into her path. I dropped into a crouch and held my palm out like a crossing guard. She stopped directly in front of me. "Miss," I said, "please don't run here. You could get hurt." She nodded sagely and walked slowly away. But once she thought that she was out of my sight, she once again took off running.

Customers engaged me again, and I wasn't able to confront her as she came around on her next lap. But when she appeared yet again, I once again stepped into her path. This time, she ducked around me and out of my view behind a tall display. I stepped around it. When she saw that I saw her, she darted off to behind another display and again stopped. After several iterations of this, I realized that she thought that we were playing Hide and Seek.

I dropped again to a crouch, stepping around and putting my arms out so that she was boxed in. "You can't run here. This isn't a playground." She nodded again, and I stood up.

"Elena!" I heard two voices call in unison, coming toward us. The girl turned and ran to the couple approaching us. The woman scooped the girl up and scolded her (I think) in a language that I couldn't identify. The man nodded toward me. "Thank you," he said. "Thank you we sorry thank you bye." They headed down the escalator to the lower floors.

By late evening, most of the customers had gone—which meant that the store seemed mostly to be occupied by the denizens of the area who use it as some sort of refuge. Tracksuit Man showed up, as always, about twenty minutes before we closed and left with about three minutes to spare.

Crutch Lady was, as usual, the last one to leave the café. Also, as usual, she headed up to the restrooms, which she knew had closed. She appeared to have given up about arguing her way in, since she saw that the entrance was guarded by the indomitable

Miss Broadway. So she headed on out, remembering, this time, to take with her the crutches that she appears not to really need. (We wonder if she's connected somehow to the guy who wandered off without his wheelchair before Christmas. Does our coffee have miraculous healing powers?)

Another woman spent well over an hour in the restroom. When she emerged, she immediately asked Miss Broadway if there were any public restrooms around and tried to engage her and, later, DJ LP, in a monologue about blood and hygiene products that neither was in a mood to hear.

Mr. Duffel was also on the fourth floor. He didn't fall asleep this time, but spent a couple of hours among the movie books speaking an energetic monologue. He has a beautiful speaking voice, and could easily get a spot on talk radio if he were a little less coherent. When he launched into an apparent demonstration, with descriptions, of what looked like a litany of movements from the martial arts, I let people know over the headset intercom. DJ LP said that that was probably OK, as long as he didn't hit anyone or knock anything over, and didn't head into the kids section.

Fortunately, he left on time. I had had trouble with him on Thursday. Each time that I let him know that we were about to close, he nodded and kept on reading. When the closing announcement came, he gradually closed his book and put it on the table... then carefully rolled up his bag of Cheetos... then opened his Walgreens bag and put the Cheetos in it... then put down the bag, stood up slowly, and picked it up again... then picked up his duffel bag... then walked a few yards over to another table... then put the Walgreens bag on the table... then put the duffel bag on the table... then picked up the Walgreens bag... then took out the Cheetos bag... then put down the Cheetos bag... then put down the Walgreens bag... then zipped open the duffel bag... then picked up the Cheetos bag... then rolled it tightly and tried to stuff it in the duffel bag... then put the Cheetos bag down... then took a sweater out of the duffel bag... then picked up the

221

Cheetos bag, unrolled it, and laid it flat inside the duffel bag...
then put the sweater in the duffel bag... then zipped up the duffel bag... then picked up the Walgreens bag... then put down the Walgreens bag... then unzipped the duffel bag... then pulled another small bag out of the Walgreens bag... ... and so on. If I hadn't been so tired, it would have seemed like some fascinating piece of minimalist theater, needing only a score by Philip Glass.

But today, he left on time, as did all the others. Many of those who shuffled out at the end of the night will be back tomorrow. And I'll be there, too, out of the breakroom, endlessly shelving. There's always more shelving to be done.

The Dancing Man

17 February 2007

The Dancing Man came sailing up the escalator in our closing hour. The sounds of a Yemenite singer, mixed with disco beats, greeted him as we tried out Madonna's new live album on the overhead system. He bounded over to Material Girl and me as we stood by the information console. "Greetings to you!" he bellowed. "God bless you all with peace and respect for your friendliness and your knowledge! God bless this country with peace and respect!" He reached out a large hand and we shook on it as he continued with more benedictions.

Finally releasing his grip, he stepped toward the listening stations. I looked around for Material Girl, who had fled surprisingly quickly, the door to the back office closing behind her.

"Do you like to dance?" he said.

I shrugged, smiling. "It's not quite in my skill set."

"Everyone can dance!" he said and shifted into a sort of shuffling Wild and Crazy Guy motion, stepping back and forth, his shoulders rolling with the rhythm and his elbows flapping as he clenched his hands close to his heart.

He was good—very good, in fact, the wackiness of his dance steps elevated by the untarnished glee he took in moving to the music. The other customers had turned and were watching him, and he welcomed their gaze. One by one, his pleasure melted their embarrassment at watching him, and they all began to smile. He gestured to several to join him. When no one did, he closed his eyes, tilted his head back, and continued to move to the music.

This is the first time that I had seen the Dancing Man in a long time. When he had first appeared, sometime last year, he would spend hours on the listening stations, often listening and dancing to the same thirty second snippet of the same song. "Best song in whole world!" he would call out to people who saw him. "Paula Cole! 'I Don't Want to Wait!' Greatest song in whole world!" He would go on about the song as long as anyone would listen to him, though he couldn't say much about it, his sentences spiraling around in greater and greater praises. I couldn't place his accent (Material Girl told me that he is from Morocco), and his slightly scrambled, rather formal English would get more loopy as he rambled on.

Watching him, I was surprised to find myself singing along with the Yemenite singer on the CD, which got even stranger glances from some of the customers.

"How do you know that song?" Material Girl asked, having snuck back from the office.

"It was a big hit on an Ofra Haza record, and sampled all over the place a while back." That was eighteen years ago. I was struck once again by the difference in time frames that I have from most of my coworkers. While I was thirty then, and it fits more or less into my vague sense of "now," she was twelve at the time, and not yet noticing more than immediate pop.

"What's it mean?" she asked.

"If the doors of heaven are closed, the doors of... um... something... will not be closed... or will not be open... or something." (According to its Wikipedia entry, it means "Even if the gates of the rich will be closed, the gates of heaven will not be closed.") "I used to know this, but can't remember what the two most important words mean anymore."

As the beat of Madonna's "Isaac" dissolved seamlessly into the next song, the Dancing Man came out of his reverie and jogged back toward us. He shook my hand again as Material Girl once again backed away. "God bless you! God bless this country with peace and respect for us! Peace and respect, yes? God bless everyone here and this country!" He turned with a flourish and, in a more directional version of his shambling dance, headed to the escalator and down to the other floors.

It's Not That Easy Drinking Green

18 March 2007

The regulars didn't show up to the store tonight. Tracksuit Guy, Mr Duffel, Opera Man, Crutch Lady and the rest all took the night off. It was St. Patrick's Day, and all the amateur drinkers and those deranged by apparently unaccustomed partying showed up in force. The expert denizens knew to keep a low profile and wait for the frenzied to stumble back to their suburbs and their SUVs.

I tried to get into work early, knowing that we were in the middle of a four afternoon stretch when getting around downtown would be screwed up. Market Street was officially closed on Saturday for the St. Patrick's Day parade, and would be officially closed again on Sunday for an anti-war march. Further anti-war events were scheduled for Friday (at least I thought there was a "die-in" planned, though I haven't seen any reporting of it) and more for Monday.

The BART was delayed coming into Berkeley, and had more delays as it went along into the city. At 3 PM, people were already stumbling on the platforms and meandering through the cars yelling. As I came up out of the BART at Powell Street, there was more of the same. Crew cut fullbacks bellowed as they rambled through the dense crowd. Parents pulled children out of the way as brawlers plowed forward and crashed into walls, attempting to show the walls who was boss. Some of them might even have believed that they succeeded.

The path uphill to the store was similarly mobbed, though it thinned as I got closer to the store—perhaps the steep hill defeated the attempts of some of them to climb. My supervisor, who was out on the square for his lunch, reported even stranger behavior: he saw several pairs of people ride into the square on bicycles. In each case, the one who wasn't driving would hop off the bike, disrobe, be photographed, dress again, and zoom out of the square. It all seemed organized, though the purpose was unclear.

I got into work a couple of minutes late. While I should have gotten a sticker from the Loss Prevention person at the door to show that I had brought in the book that I was carrying from outside (so it wouldn't be a problem when I tried to leave with it), he was tied up trying to explain something to a customer. I went into the office, got a sticker from a manager, and proceeded up to the music floor.

When I got up to the floor, the other workers told me that things were quiet—and then three of my usual avid customers came charging at me from different directions at once, each wanting to deal only with me. One wanted my opinion on some DVDs of Wagner's *Götterdamerung*, none of which I had seen. Another was asking about Joshua Bell's recordings of Kreisler, quite loudly—though he is a choir director, he seems to have no control over the volume of his speaking voice. The third just wanted to say hello, but was very insistent on it.

What other customers there were weren't too rambunctious, but many seemed either unusually clumsy or to be moving stiffly. As customer after customer got to the registers, I caught the whiff of beer on the breath of many. Several laughed too loudly at jokes, or tried hard to appear nonchalant about large purchases. Others were having a bit of trouble figuring out how money worked. And a large number shared the excessively formality that people use in trying to show that they aren't, in fact, trashed.

Other than that, though, there was little impact up on our floor. (I'm told that things were different at the front door, as the Loss Prevention folks had to convince a continuing stream of people that they couldn't come into a bookstore while brandishing steins of beer.)

I got an interesting question later in the day. A woman was walking around, picking up CDs, looking very closely at their covers, then putting them down. She didn't seem to notice when I had asked her if she could find anything. But eventually she came up to me and asked if I worked there. (That I was on the store phone and was wearing a large badge might have suggested to her that I did.)

"Do you know jazz?" she asked.

"Somewhat," I said. "What are you looking for?"

"I'm trying to find an album. I think it was recorded in 1957. I had a cover by the same guy who did this." Digging into her bag, she pulled out the CD cover booklet of Dave Brubeck's *Time Out.*

I was stumped. Looking through the book, I tried in vain to find out who did the cover, but came up cold. "I don't have a clue," I said. "The best thing you could do is get online, and search for 'dave brubeck time out cover art.' Come to think of it, it may be Joan Miro. Once you find that, search on the artist's name, and it may take you to—"

I paused, as a image suddenly flashed through my head. Recognizing it, I stepped around to the next jazz aisle and pulled out a copy of Mingus's *Mingus Ah Um.* "Is this it?" I asked.

She took the CD from me, looked closely at it, and then back at me. "How the hell did you figure that out? You must have every album cover in the store in your head."

"Actually, someone else was looking for this same album a few hours ago, and I saw it then, so I must have still had it cached in

RAM." I immediately realized that she probably had no idea what "cached in RAM" would mean, but she didn't look confused. She thanked me, and gleefully ran off with the CD.

(I just tried the search strategy that I suggested to her, and, to my relief, it did work. I was wrong about Joan Miro though. He did Brubeck's next album, *Time Further Out*. These covers were by Neil Fujita.)

The earlier customer who was looking for the Mingus CD had originally asked for a Miles Davis album named *So What*. It took a bit of doing to convince him that what he really wanted was *Kind of Blue*. (And I just found online an apparent album named *So What*. but it looks like a bootleg.) He had just started reading John Szwed's biography, which is named *So What*, and wanted to get the corresponding album. We went over to the jazz books, and I flipped through discographies until I was able to convince him that no official album of that name existed.

Another frequent customer, who was usually angry about something, showed up later, looking for a recording by Leonard Bernstein of Beethoven's 5th Symphony. (She was pleased to have gotten the main riff as her cellphone ringtone, and wanted to have the rest of the piece.)

The one recording that we had in stock also had Beethoven's 4th Symphony and Egmont Overture. She had looked at it skeptically. "It has another symphony and this Eg- Eg- this Eg thing on it, too? Are you sure it has the whole 5th symphony?"

I had assured her that it did, and asked if she would like to get it.

"Oh, no," she replied. "I had already ordered it from you, and you have it for me downstairs. I just wanted to see if it was the right thing before I waited in line for it." She zoomed off before I could explain to her that there were several different releases of Bernstein's Beethoven's 5th, and that there was no certainly that what she had ordered was the same one.

When I took my ten-minute break toward the end of the day, she showed up again as I tried to flee for the breakroom. As usual, she was annoyed. "This is not the same recording!" She handed me the CD that she had ordered. It did, indeed, have the 5th on it, but also had an interview with Bernstein about the work. "This has talking on it! I do not want to hear someone who's dead talking about the music. That's just too creepy!"

I looked at the CD, and at the price sticker. "We can certainly exchange it. This one is the same price as the one that I showed you earlier."

"Where can I find it? Where were we when you showed it to me?"

"It was up in the Beethoven area, near the beginning of classical, in the... um... Come on upstairs, I'll get it for you."

"But aren't you headed to your break or lunch or something?"

"Yes, but this takes priority."

"Oh! I wish more stores had service like this!"

What I didn't tell her was that I had gotten utterly flummoxed trying to describe where the CD was. I have trouble with "left" and "right," especially in mapping the words to the actual directions when I'm not actually pointing at something. So odds were very strong that any directions that I would have given her would have been incomplete or just plain wrong.

We got upstairs, and I quickly got the CD from the rack for her. "If you bring it back downstairs to the ground floor registers, they can do the exchange for you."

"Here," she said, "let me give you this for it." She reached into her bag and pulled out a very well-made, but obviously fake million dollar bill. "Now don't leave this lying around. People have a way of running off with them."

Fortunately, all the customers cleared out of the store fairly early, and we actually had reshelved all the books by closing time. We zoomed out soon after we closed. I even managed to get down to the station in time for the last BART and didn't have to take the bus. A coworker was glad that I accompanied her down the hill; Powell Street was still full of revelers, some of whom she had found threatening when they had gotten an early start on the drinking the night before.

The BART took longer than usual. It was crowded, and several people had trouble understanding that this was the last train and that they had to board it. Some also had some trouble getting into the train and remaining standing or sitting once the train lurched into motion.

A lot of people laughed and talked loudly, some cursing volubly, as the trip progressed. A few couples also appeared to be a bit more avidly intertwined than might be appropriate on public transit.

By the time we approached Berkeley, most had gotten off. The person sitting alone in front of me alternated between stern grimaces and brief explosions of laughter, sometimes pounding on his bicycle and shaking his head as if in response to music, though he didn't appear to be wearing headphones. Despite the shamrock stamped on the back of his hand, though, I recognized him as the one of the regulars from the train rides. As I got off the train and his sudden howl faded away, I felt assured that things were getting back to normal.

An Ear for the Odd

25 May 2007

I've been trying out various music overhead at work, limited, of course, by what we stock. I think I've figured out an interesting pattern: if I play popular music overhead, few people notice (except to complain when it's too loud). But when I play different music, especially that with a sound that is immediately unusual though not annoying and which draws people in, they'll ask about it, and odds are much higher that they'll buy it. People are immediately curious when I play Azam Ali, Loreena McKennitt, Tomasz Stanko, or Steve Reich.

One interesting pattern is that when we play early Leonard Cohen albums, where his singing was a fairly common-sounding tenor, they only get a little interest, mostly from people who recognize them. But when we play his later work, where his voice is a gravelly whisper and the other elements are arrayed to leave room for it, people immediately head for the "Now Playing" rack. The first time that we played disc 2 of *The Essential Leonard Cohen*, we sold all three copies that we had in stock before the CD ended. When we got it back in stock, I put on disc 2 again, and we sold a copy within two minutes, during the opening song, "Everybody Knows."

I've also noticed (and confirmed by speaking with the CD folks at other stores) that more and more people are failing to find CDs that we stock because they are assuming that they are organized by the artists' first name. At first, I thought that this was just kinda dumb, since everything everywhere is organized by last name, but then I had an epiphany: many people now most commonly see lists of artists on their iPods or in iTunes, and unless one takes fairly arduous measures to change things, the artists are organized by their first names. So we're stuck with a fairly annoying partial paradigm shift.

Silences on Display

27 June 2007

Seeing that the store had gotten a copy of John Cage's *Silence* in stock, I kidded my supervisor that I should put up a display with that and some blank CDs. Thinking about it further, though, it seemed like a less crazy idea. So we now have a display with the book, two blank journals, a box of clear empty CD cases, a foreign film called *The Silence*, Simon and Garfunkel's *Sounds of Silence*, a book from the Religion section on silence and solitude, and a sign that says "(silence)." It looks good, and our General Manager says that it's one of the best displays he's seen in the store. Running with a sublime, goofy idea works again.

CHAPTER 24

Is Red Louder Than a Square?

2 July 2007

The customer was fidgeting with a DVD when I came over to him. "Can I help you find anything?"

"Actually, I have a question for you," he said. He spoke quickly, not quite agitated but clearly wired, with an accent that sounded vaguely West African or Caribbean, though I couldn't pin it down further than that. "What is the difference in relative mass between this DVD and an empty DVD?"

I figured that this was somehow going to lead to a question about shipping charges. "Well, DVD's don't weigh very much, so an empty case won't weigh much less than a case that has a DVD in it."

"No, no, not an empty DVD case. An empty DVD, without information on it."

"Do you mean a blank DVD versus a recorded one?"

"Yes, yes, precisely, an empty DVD versus, as you say, recorded."

I thought for a moment. "There should be no difference at all." (Actually, I wasn't quite sure if the change in the die caused by the laser actually made any difference in the mass, but I don't think so.)

"Aha!" he said gleefully. "So Einstein was indeed wrong!"

Thinking rapidly and deeply about this revelation, I responded with an erudite "Huh?"

He walked over to our display of blank DVDs, picked one up, and waved it in the air. "This DVD is empty. It has no information. Correct?"

"That's close enough to true," I said.

He waved the recorded DVD in his other hand. "And this DVD is full of information. Correct?"

"Yes, it is."

"Yet they weigh exactly the same amount!" Apparently he had taken into account the weight of the substantial booklet in the recorded DVD's case.

"OK... But Einstein?"

"Einstein!" he crowed. "Einstein declared that E equals m c squared, that energy and mass are the same thing. Yet this contains information, which is clearly a thing, yet you say that it makes no difference to the mass."

"Well. It does have more information. But information doesn't necessarily weigh anything."

"Yes! And therefore Einstein was wrong!"

I was growing more puzzled. "Look, if there's a piece of paper with a bunch of random letters on it, and another piece of paper with the letters arranged into a poem, what is the difference in what they weigh?"

"You say that there is no difference. But Einstein said that there must be."

"What does Einstein have to do with it?"

"The information is either a thing, in which case it has mass, or has moved the items around, in which case it is an energy, which should be converted to mass, like ice turning to water. And a lecture that I just came from said that all twentieth century science, especially Einstein, was wrong, because they ignored the presence of information."

OK, so this guy had just fallen off the deep end of science without having taken Physics 101. "But Information Science is a huge field."

"Physics ignores it," he said. "It is wrong."

"So you're saying that if something contains information, it must be heavier than something that is not."

"Correct!"

I picked up five CDs from a display and put them on a table near us, shifting them around. "OK, here are five CDs. They are in alphabetical order. Would you say that that is more information than they contain on their own?"

"Obviously," he said.

Using my best Three Card Monte skills, I scrambled the order of the discs. "Now do you see that they are not in order?"

"Yes, of course."

"Do you say that they now weigh more or less than they did before?"

"If there was an order to them, they must have weighed more, and you dissipated the mass in the energy of scrambling them."

"Hmm, how can I explain this?... OK, information exists, but it doesn't make things heavier or, um, warmer. It's irrelevant to mass or energy."

"If it is a quality that exists it must be expressible as mass or energy, or Einstein was wrong."

At this point I really wished I could reach over and pull Douglas Hofstadter out from behind a pillar. "Look," I said, "It boils down to a simple analogy. Tell me: Is red louder than a square?"

He actually stopped fidgeting for a moment. "That question cannot have a meaningful answer."

"Precisely!" I said. "And there can be no meaningful answer as to the weight of information, since information is not a mass-or-energy kind of thing." By this point I was plowing ahead on my own momentum, vaguely aware that I was utterly winging it and wasn't entirely sure that I wasn't, in some high-level scientific way, dead wrong. But I tried not to let it show.

"So Einstein was wrong!" he said again.

"What do you believe that Einstein said about this?"

"Einstein said that e equals m c squared, that energy is the same thing as matter and that that's the only thing in the universe."

I started to get what he meant. "OK, he did say that they can be essentially the same thing. But I don't think he said that they were the only things in the universe."

"What else might he have believed that there would be?"

It was time for a mad theoretical leap. "As you might recall, Einstein said that God does not play dice with the universe."

"I recall that he did, yes."

"So he must have allowed for the possible existence, in some sense, of God, correct?"

"I suppose that he did."

"So is God matter or is God energy?"

He stared blankly for a moment, his hands dropping to his sides. "God must be neither. So... Einstein said that there was matter, energy, and... God? And God is above them?"

"Well, I think he said that there might be a God. And I don't know if God would be above them, or alongside." I gestured, moving my hands in skew lines.

"Alongside... not... maybe..."

"And thus information is alongside energy or matter, and doesn't affect weight."

He stood silent, his face moving between epiphany and breakdown.

Suddenly, another customer ran up and stood between us. "Joe! I loved the discs you sold me last night! Now you have to find me the Brian Eno, Gerald Markoe, and Tony Scott discs again!"

"OK," I said. I looked up at the Einstein guy and said "Excuse me," but he didn't seem to notice. And by the time that I found the discs for the other customer, he had disappeared.

Later, a coworker who had been standing nearby said that we had been getting rather loud in the conversation. "I thought you were arguing about a bogus coupon or something until I listened to you. Then I thought of getting involved, but couldn't find a way to wedge in."

"I wish you had," I said. "Your science is probably less rusty than mine." As with most of my coworkers, he had probably taken a science class a quarter-century more recently than I had.

My supervisor then came over. "You do know that that's the guy who was in here a few months ago complaining that we had conspired with the FBI to steal his jacket, right?"

"It's that guy? That sort of makes his not making sense make sense."

"It figures that he'd come to you."

I sighed. "They all come to me. I'm the freak magnet."

I had a few more weird people during the day, and there will be more in the next few. Whether or not these have an effect, it is just about the full moon, and it's the first of the month, when many of our regulars get their government checks. So we'll be seeing more, with more odd encounters. Perhaps I'd better brush up on relativity, just in case.

CHAPTER 25

Exit Music (For a Customer)

30 July 2007

As the evening dragged on, several of us wondered aloud over our headsets once again why we were open so late on a Sunday night. Almost all of the paying customers had wandered off by nine, two hours before closing. The remaining swarm consisted mostly of jet-lagged European tourists who would tend to wander about and not buy things, and of our regular denizens. Most of those were draped over our most comfortable chairs, either sleeping, staring belligerently at any who dared to approach them, or nattering to people we couldn't see.

Our supervisors gave the ritual announcements, starting an hour before closing, to make sure that people had time to pull their stuff together and leave on time. They even made more announcements than usual, since some of the people seemed especially resistant to leaving.

Right after the ten minute warning, just as I thought I had cleared the floor for the night, a woman came up the escalator, dressed in a sharp business suit and carrying a briefcase. She stopped after walking ahead by a few steps, and went into the usual bird-like head bobbing of someone trying to figure out quickly where we've put things.

"Can I help you?" I asked.

"I need the Paul McCartney," she said. "The new one. The latest one."

"That'll be over here," I said, walking over to a display. It wasn't there. "Or definitely over here," I continued, heading back to the McCartney bin in the Pop/Rock section. I pulled it from the bin, handed it to her, and began to walk back with her to the escalators.

"Is it good?" she asked. "Is it a good one? It's not for me. It's for my dad. Will he like it?"

"It's good," I said. "It's a good Paul McCartney album. No one's going to go 'Oh, wow, I never expected Paul McCartney to do this! ', but if you liked the last one —and I liked the last one a lot—you'll like this one."

"OK," she said, then slowed and turned to face me. "Um, would you have…" she paused. "What music do you have for someone who's dying? I mean, he's dying right now, and I want to have music for him… to have… when he goes."

"What does he like to listen to?" I asked.

"Classical. Jazz. Choral. Instruments. World. Chants. You know…" she replied.

"Well, I can think of one thing right off," I said. "I read an article in the New Yorker a while back about music playing in hospices. It said that this piece— " I pulled a CD of Arvo Pärt's "Tabula Rasa" from the composer's rack "—was the favorite music for people who… were there."

"For dying people? Can I listen to it?"

I took her over to a listening station and showed her how to scan a disc and listen to excerpts. She listened to the snippet that we could play of "Tabula Rasa," nodded, and took off the headphones. "This is good. What else would you suggest?"

I got her the Trio Mediaeval's *Soir, Dit Elle.* "This is a favorite of mine. Three soprano voices, very spare, drifting and winding around each other in the silence."

"I like that," she said. "I'll give it a listen. Do you have any chants that would be good, Tibetan or Hindu or something like that?"

I went over to the world music bins as she listened to the Trio Mediaeval and pulled out some suggestions. She listened to several. She immediately liked Lama Gyurme's *Rain of Blessings: Varja Chants,* and turned down Nawang Khechog's *Tibetan Meditation Music* since it had flutes instead of chanting. I stepped away while she was listening to those and pulled out Pat Metheny's *One Quiet Night,* Deva Premal's *The Essence,* and *Sacred Tibetan Chant* by the Monks of Sherab Ling Monastery (though I ended up not suggesting it to her as I remembered that it gets kind of raucous toward the end).

When I got back to her, our manager was announcing over the loudspeakers that we were closed. The customer appeared to be talking to herself, but I realized, as I returned to her, that what I had thought was an earring was a Bluetooth earpiece for her phone. "OK... OK... I'll be there... So he's... OK... So I'll be there soon... Bye."

Our manager was now asking the employees to clear the floors. "I'm going to be a moment," I said over the headset. "I'm still with a customer." I decided that I was going to give this customer as much time as she needed.

She decided to get the Metheny and the Deva Premal. "Thanks," she said. "This is... we didn't expect this. He just... and I had to find the music, and I..."

"I understand," I said. "I lost my father about a year ago, and I can feel where you are."

"Well, thanks so much for... for this," she said.

I nodded. "It's an honor to be able to help you."

She headed down the escalator. I got on the loudspeaker, announced that the fourth floor was clear, and listened as each of the remaining floors were declared clear as she descended.

I moved around the floor, putting away the CDs that she didn't get, and found myself shaky and tearing up. This had been more difficult than I had thought as I was doing it, and I felt like I had been involved in a kind of sacred responsibility.

On my way down, I told a coworker about the customer's search.

"Wouldn't you just want to play whatever music the person liked most?" she asked.

"From what I've learned," I said, "that's not quite it. Sometimes you don't want anything with too strong a hook or a rhythm. If a person is in the process of going, music like that can get in the way, and can block some of the emotions." (I recall that there's a story in the Talmud about just such a thing.)

"Hmm," she said. "Not something I would have imagined."

I got down to the basement and finally clocked out. My manager was down there, waiting to close the building. I told him what had happened. "What an end to the day," I said.

"And what a night," he replied.

I leaned against the wall, regaining my balance, as I waited for the elevator. Thinking back on all the annoyances of the day, I returned to the image and emotions of that final customer. And I realized that, after all the problems, this is why we are here.

Postscript

17 February 2011

By the time you read this, the store in this book will be gone.

Yesterday, as we were preparing this book for publication, the company announced that two hundred of its stores were closing as part of a bankruptcy reorganization. The store on San Francisco's Union Square was one of them. I don't yet know whether the chain as a whole will survive and continue, but by the time you read this, that question may have been answered.

Not long after the events of this book, I moved on to another store in the chain. A group of us wanted to create a Jewish arts colony in the suburbs of Cleveland, and I transferred to a store here. The colony project failed, but I stayed on. The new store is doing relatively well, and wasn't among this first wave of closings.

The book and music business now barely resembles what it was just five years ago. The CD selection at the store dwindled as the market for placing physical CDs in stores collapsed. Our total CD collection is now smaller than our classical collection was when I started. The book business, to a great extent, has done the same.

The day of the big physical store, having all things for all people immediately in stock, seems to have passed. The place of the dedicated in-person salesman (what a customer once called "a sommelier for music") may be reverting to its previous form: the small, focused shop where the salesman knows his or her community well, and has the power and flexibility to order and stock just what that particular store's customers would enjoy.

Though a lot about my job has changed, and moments of connection seem harder to find, I still try to keep an ear out for them in each day's work. I'm still writing about them each working day (give or take a few) on my blog, *The Path of the Bookseller*, at www.josephzitt.com/blog/.

I don't know how things will stand by the time that you read this. My new store and the company may or may not survive. I may or may not be out of a job. (If I am, would any of you need a dynamite book and music seller?)

But I hope to be continuing to do that which I do best: helping the people that I meet to find whatever they are seeking and to discover the items, ideas, and connections that they will love.

After all, this is why we're here.

About the Author

After working for many years as a technical writer and programmer, Joseph Zitt became a book and music seller in San Francisco in 2002. His other writings and recordings emerge from experience with computer systems, religious studies, and vocal improvisation. They include the books *Surprise Me With Beauty: the Music of Human Systems*, *Shekhinah: the Presence*, *The Rounds*, and *The Book of Voices*. He now works proudly as a bookseller outside of Cleveland, Ohio. You can find more about his books and other projects at www.josephzitt.com.